VAY

Owain Glyndŵr's Way

Richard Sale

GWASG CARREG GWALCH

ISBN: 0-86381-690-8

Cover design: Alan Jones

First published in 2001 by
Gwasg Carreg Gwalch, 12 Iard yr Orsaf, Llanrwst, Wales LL26 0EH
℡ 01492 642031   📠 01492 641502
🖱 books@carreg-gwalch.co.uk   Internet: www.carreg-gwalch.co.uk

CONTENTS

INTRODUCTION

In the Marble Hall of Cardiff's City Hall – reserved for heroes of the Welsh nation – is a statue of Owain Glyndŵr. Here also are St David, Dafydd ap Gwilym, Esgob Morgan and Hywel Dda.

Owain Glyndŵr lived during the latter half of the fourteenth and the early years of the fifteenth century. In those first years of the fifteenth century he led a revolt against the English, during the course of which the land of Wales was devastated by the 'scorched earth' policy of the English king and, to a lesser extent, by the followers of Glyndŵr. It was a long and hard battle against English colonialism in his country. He provided rewarding successes at first, but his resources were limited and he finally vanished into the unknown and into his land's legends. Not once was he betrayed, and the aims he set out for himself have been the cornerstones of Welsh modern history. After six hundred years, his dreams are slowly becoming reality.

This book however is not a biography nor does it try to explain why Owain Glyndŵr is Wales' national hero. He is revered as a symbol of freedom and the father of a new era of nationhood in Wales, even though as the final embers of his revolt died away, Wales was oppressed by punitive laws, enacated to try to ensure that never again would the Welsh rise to trouble the English overlords. Wales was left in slavery

This book does not try to explain this paradox, for the answer lies buried in the psyche of the Welsh. What it can and does do, however, is to set out the history of the revolt and place it in the context of the history of Wales both before and after Glyndŵr. The aims and conduct of the rebellion are set down, so that the reader can form his own opinion of the judgement that the Welsh have made on this man.

But in order fully to explore Glyndŵr's aims, and Welsh hopes at the time of the rebellion, it is necessary to understand something of Wales. To do that, there is no better way than to follow the route of Britain's newest National Trail, one that closely follows the old route waymarked originally by Powys County Council. The Trail starts at Knighton, on Offa's Dyke and still on the English border, near the battlefield of Pilleth where Glyndŵr had his most decisive victory. It visits Abbey Cwmhir where Llywelyn II lies buried, and the uplands of Pumlumon where Glyndŵr raised his standard and also won his first victory over the English. The route then continues to Machynlleth where Owain held the first parliament of his free Wales, before heading towards the Welsh upland again, this time the Berwyn mountains and Llyn Efyrnwy. Beyond is Mathrafal, home of the Welsh Princes of Powys from whom Owain was descended, then Welshpool with its Red Castle, symbolic of Norman England. Map references within the text refer to Ordnance Survey maps (see Appendix 1).

In addition to following the history of Owain's revolt, Glyndŵr's Way passes through some of the finest scenery in mid-Wales. While this area does not have the grandeur of the mountains in Snowdonia nor the stark beauty of the scarp slopes of the Brecon Beacons National Park, it does boast the wooded vales of Radnor, the Clywedog valley, the unspoilt areas of old Montgomeryshire and, along the Afon Dyfi, perhaps the loveliest river valley in Wales.

Those who travel Glyndŵr's Way will also explore a country rich in history, myth and legend, and see some of the finest scenery in Britain at first hand. Perhaps too they will understand a little more of this most enigmatic, yet charismatic, of Welsh leaders.

Part One
Before and After Glyndŵr

From Celtic Wales
to Norman times

In common with the remainder of Britain, Wales has been inhabited spasmodically for perhaps a quarter of a million years. Settlement has not been continuous, however, for the population had to move south periodically to escape the Ice Ages.

When the ice finally retreated peoples of the Neolithic cultures occupied the coastal plain of Wales and Ynys Môn (Anglesey), leaving the upland central dome alone: they did not have the technology either to tame its wilderness or to survive its climate. Later prehistoric cultures did colonise the central area, making occasional use of the high land for ceremonial purposes. The route described in this book visits a burial site of the late Bronze Age, its barrows perched on a spur of the high plateau so that they dominate the surrounding countryside. It also passes close to a stone circle, one of those most enigmatic of sites, also associated with the earliest metal-using peoples.

In central Europe - now known as the Celtic cradle because the two early or proto-Celtic peoples are named from representative sites in that area (Hallstatt in Austria and La Tène in Switzerland) – the Bronze Age was slowly giving way to the Iron Age. The change was gradual: at first there were a few iron implements, later more and then finally all tools were of iron. It is likely too that the Bronze Age folk were not wiped out by a sudden influx of iron users, but that there was an evolution to an iron-using culture, perhaps with the integration of some external peoples.

In Wales the same thing appears to have happened. In South Wales a site has revealed contemporary bronze and iron objects and the fairy story of the lady of Llyn y Fan Fach in the Brecon Beacons National Park has strong overtones of the meeting of two cultures without the conquest of one by the other.

But while the iron cultures may have been integrated into the existing Bronze Age system, the country – and that includes the whole of Britain rather than just Wales – became dominated by the Celtic peoples of. This domination was reinforced by many subsequent invasions or resettlements. The early newcomers could have been settlers in search of new lands, or possibly refugees escaping from the invasions of southerly warlike tribes. Later newcomers were definitely tribes on the run from the Romans who were advancing northward in search of security for Rome's northern border, lands to exploit and people to tax.

The Romans gave the people the name by which they are now known, using Keltoi as their general term, interchangeable with Galli for the inhabitants of Gaul (France). It is from the Romans that we have our first picture of the Celts, who had no written form to their language and therefore have no written history. The Romans were unimpressed. True the Celts were good in battle, but they were savages – their leaders forever having their praises sung by paid sycophants, their priestly cult a murderous bunch of pagans. To learn of a people's positive qualities there is never any point in asking their enemies, and the Romans would have been unusual had they wanted to portray the Celts in anything other than a poor light. That said and with due allowance for the consequent distortion, the Roman criticisms are founded on truth – as they saw it. The Celts were indeed a warlike people whose culture – as seen in Wales – seems to have thrived on, almost depended upon, tribal warfare. The tribal leaders did indeed have a stock of bards singing their praises but, in the absence of a written language, oral tradition was the only way of keeping in touch with the past. Moreover, in a military society the need to maintain a leader and a ruling elite necessitates enthusiasm for their warrior qualities and those of their ancestors. As for the Druids, the Celtic priesthood, no evidence for blood sacrifice exists other than that offered by the Romans, and even if they did practise such sacrifice they were not alone in doing so. Two thousand years ago the Celts were as much children of their times as we are of our own today, and ours is hardly a bloodless society. Recently it has become fashionable to assign all manner of ancient wisdom to megalith builders and the Druids, though the latter certainly did not build any megalithic sites, despite the charade now carried out at Stonehenge on Midsummer's Day: it may well be that they were more in tune with their environment than we are, but as for being in touch with a higher plane – when cornered by the Romans in Ynys Môn the Druids answered by cursing the advancing legionaries in ritual fashion. It was ancient wisdom against the short sword. It was no contest.

The Romans had arrived in Britain in AD 43 to find a tribal system fully established, similar to that which they had already encountered in mainland Europe. Indeed their knowledge of the Celts, acquired in Europe, assisted them in their conquest. The Celtic tribes fought each other almost continuously, an endless series of battles between alliances which formed and reformed as personalities rose and fell in their respective hierarchies. Any king who managed by means fair or foul to create any semblance of order or unity, had his work undone immediately he died. This was inevitable as *gavelkind* was the custom in the Celtic tribes, the lands of the father being divided equally between the sons. As soon as this happened the sons would fight each other or else another tribe, seeing its chance to rise up the ladder, would overthrow one or other son. Only rarely were the Celts able to unite to resist an outside power, and then usually to present merely a short-term united front.

Prior to the Roman invasion Britain was split up into a

number of tribal holdings, but the leader that prompted the invasion and offered the stiffest opposition was Cunobelinus, the Cymbeline of Shakespeare's play. In AD 40 the king had banished a son, Amminius. Why is not certain, but it was probably for plotting rebellion, and Amminius went to Rome for help against his family. By the time Aulus Plautius arrived with his army, Cunobelinus was dead and the opposing army was led by two other sons, Togodumnus and Caratacus. Togodumnus was killed early in the campaign, but Caratacus stoutly resisted the invaders – suffering defeat after defeat, but always rising to resist again a little further to the west. In what is now Wales, but what was then merely another part of the Celtic homeland, Caratacus stirred the Silures of the south and the Ordovices of the north to join him to throw back the Romans. Around AD 51 there was a final battle, the exact site of which is unknown, but it was in central Wales near the Shropshire border and Caratacus was captured. The Romans must have been somewhat dismayed when the Celtic leader escaped and fled north to raise another army. The Brigantes there may well have helped him, but their queen Cartimandua – either pro-Roman already or sensing which way the wind was blowing – handed him over to the Romans. She received her reward from them, even if she did not receive the enthusiastic support of her people, and Caratacus was sent in chains to Rome. There he was paraded as a captive savage and is reputed to have lectured the Roman senate on their idiotic attitude towards those who opposed them: 'If you want to rule the world, does it follow that everyone else welcomes enslavement... Spare me, and I shall be an everlasting token of your mercy.' The Romans were impressed by this noble savage and, although he was held until his death, Caratacus lived in honourable captivity, if such a condition exists. In Wales he was enthusiastically taken up as a hero. After all, he was Celtic even if he did have the misfortune to have been born near London. Wales is full of references to him, usually as Caradog – the

Welsh form of his name – and there are many Caer Caradogs where that last battle was reputedly fought.

Following the subjugation of the Welsh tribes, Wales – as with the rest of Britain as far as Hadrian's Wall – settled down to a long period of Romanised living. This came to an end when the Romans departed in the first quarter of the fifth century, no longer able to police and safeguard this far corner of their Empire from Irish and Pictish raiders. What followed immediately upon their departure was astonishing.

Britain had lived through nearly four centuries of Roman domination, yet virtually as the last Roman legionary shook off the British dust from his sandal and went on board ship, the ancient tribes were regrouping around new kings all of whom could trace their line back to pre-Roman times. The bards returned to sing of ancestral deeds: the Celtic traditions had returned to the land.

However, while it is to their credit that the Celts had maintained their culture in the face of occupation, it is sad that they had learned so little from the Romans. Britain had been occupied by a people with one name but a multitude of backgrounds. The Hard Knott fort for example, perhaps the furthest-flung bastion in the whole Roman Empire, buried deep in the hills of the Lake District, had been built by troops from the Adriatic (Dalmatian) coast. What the Romans had taught their subject powers was that unity was all. TH White has Merlin say in *The Once and Future King*: 'I could never stomach these nationalists. If you keep on dividing you end up as a collection of monkeys throwing nuts at each other.' Though written many centuries later as dialogue for another time, the sentiments were as appropriate in fifth-century Britain as at any other period.

Around 450 Vortigern, a Brythonic king, was troubled by typical tribal pressures and asked Saxons from Europe to come to his aid. They came, they helped, and then they stayed. Later Vortigern, known to the Welsh as Gwrtheyrn, fled to Wales to avoid the new peril he had imported.

Once in Britain the Saxons pushed steadily westward, exploiting this tribal-conflict weakness of the Celts, stopping or retreating occasionally when the Celts fought back and then marching west again. In 577 Cuthwine and Ceawlin fought and killed three British kings – Conmail, Condidan and Farinmail – at the battle of Dyrham near Bristol, thus thrusting a Saxon wedge between the Brythons of Wales and northern England and those of south-west England. The latter were pushed westward and became the Cornish, maintaining until very recently a language that has great similarities to Welsh. Forty years passed and Aethelfrith of Northumbria won a bloody battle at Chester, defeating an army led by a grandson of Brochfael Ysgythrog. Brochfael was a feared leader whose arms had been three severed heads. After the battle Aethelfrith slaughtered thousands of monks, claiming that by praying for a Welsh victory they had fought as much as those who had held swords. This was a decisive victory. The battle cut off the Welsh of Wales from those of the Old North. Cymru had been formed, the people of the country having a common bond and referring to themselves as Cymry, 'fellow countryman'. The name Wales and Welsh are Saxon: Wallas – 'foreigners'. It has a common root with *Valais* in Switzerland, *Walloon* in Belgium and *Vlach* in Romania.

The Saxons stopped, roughly speaking, at the current border that still separates Wales from England. This roughly follows the dyke built by the Saxon king Offa, probably to stop incursions from the Welsh into his newly formed kingdom. At first sight this appears ridiculous since it was the Saxons who were the oppressors but they flinched from the difficulties of fighting in upland Wales and therefore did no more than mount punitive expeditions. A power struggle between rival Saxon leaders then relieved the pressure on the Welsh, allowing them to mount raids that were short and bloody and followed by a quick dash back to the safety of the hills. Offa's Dyke may have been built to put an end to all that, though some experts maintain that the dyke was also a negotiated border and trading line.

West of the dyke a number of kingdoms had been rapidly established when the Romans departed and, with changing borders due to the ebb and flow of rival kings, they remained approximately the same for nearly a thousand years. Gwynedd held the lands of what is now the Snowdonia National Park and the granary of Ynys Môn, making up a readily defensible and highly self-sufficient kingdom. In Wales as a whole Gwynedd invariably held power, or its balance. To the east and south of Gwynedd lay Powys, while to the south-west were the small kingdoms of Ceredigion, Dyfed and Ystrad Tywi, occasionally unified as Deheubarth. In the south-east were Brycheiniog and Buellt, and below them Morgannwg and Gwent.

The kings of Gwynedd commence – in any plausible form that is, since bardic tradition usually pushed a ruler's ancestry back towards the Creation – with Cunedda, known as Wledig (the ruler), who lived in the early fifth century. Cunedda was followed by Cadwallon, the first of many kings whose name takes the prefix *cad* – battle. After Cadwallon came Maelgwn Gwynedd, and at this point history begins to deal with real people rather than misty figures. Maelgwn was a man of huge physical stature and an apparently limitless capacity for violence. As was usual though, he was beloved of the bards and hard, but not cruel, to his subjects. It is with Maelgwn too that we reach those other architects of the Welsh nation, the Celtic Christian saints. Maelgwn gave land to Curig, an Irish missionary, for the creation of a *llan* – a sacred spot where the holy man and his followers lived. Not surprisingly, the land was at Llangurig beside the Afon Gŵy (Wye), on the edge of Pumlumon, and as even the most cursory glance at a Welsh map shows, Wales has many other *llannau* (the plural of llan) dedicated to numerous saints. St David, Dewi Sant, was active about forty years later.

Maelgwn and Curig would have made a curious pair, the

15

one a former soldier turned saint, the other a soldier in every need of his path to heaven being smoothed. In AD 547 Maelgwn 'beheld the Yellow Plague through the Keyhole of the church door and forthwith died'.

These early kings ruled a land that had changed little throughout many centuries, for despite the Saxon horde there were few refugees in Wales, the kingdoms there being untouched by the invader's hand. And so they continued, until the rise of Rhodri Fawr in the mid-ninth century. Before Rhodri it is doubtful if any king had succeeded in unifying the country, and although Rhodri himself did not in fact do so, at least he showed what could be achieved by unity.

Rhodri succeeded his father Merfyn to the kingship of Gwynedd in 844, and assumed leadership of Powys when his uncle died heirless in 854. Next he married Angharad of Ceredigion and succeeded to that throne when her brother died in 873. But he never managed to control the southern kingdoms, and must have rued their absence during his almost continual battles with Danes trying to settle the western coast of Wales. Finally, in 877, he died in battle. His kingdom was divided between his sons and Wales was splintered again.

However, Rhodri's sons did leave one gift for posterity. Intent on augmenting their own riches, they attacked and plundered the southern part of the country. The kings of the smaller states sought help from the English ruler, the mighty Alfred, and in return for agreeing to become vassals of the English crown they received his protection. Alfred attacked the north and though he lost the battle of Conwy it was obvious to Rhodri's sons that they could not hope to win or even to survive a war with the English. They too therefore became vassals, thus giving England a legal claim to the whole of Wales. Once again the Welsh flair for 'divide and fight' had been their undoing.

In time of peril from stronger neighbours, this vassal status to the English crown was useful to the kings of Wales. But when peace came it was irksome, though never sufficiently so for them to combine and throw out the English. As time went on the English, in touch with continental trends and with, by comparison, virtually unlimited resources, became increasingly difficult to remove.

In the first half of the tenth century Hywel Dda came to rule the kingdom of Deheubarth and turned his attentions to the power house of Wales: the north. He took Gwynedd when their king died in battle with England and then took Powys by force. He is remembered for his coding of Welsh law, a coding that lasted until medieval times. The laws gave women property rights a thousand years ahead of England. In the law code everything had its value – a good mouser cat was worth a sheep, for example – and all things were defined: gold plate had to be 'as thick as the nail of a ploughman who has been a ploughman for seven years'. And since money was scarce, fines could be paid in cattle. The laws of Hywel Dda were benign, liberal and just, and their application gave the prospect of a unity based on firm justice.

Following Hywel's death the Welsh kingdoms were in a confused and strife-torn state for almost a century until Gruffudd ap Llywelyn, a descendant of Hywel, finally achieved a united Wales. He then entered into a treaty with the border earls of England, marrying Ealdgyth, daughter of Earl Aelfgar. Unfortunately the ambitious Earl Harold Godwinson convinced Edward the Confesser that Gruffudd was plotting an eastward expansion and invaded Wales on the king's behalf. Gruffudd was pursued to Gwynedd, but for once the Snowdonia mountains failed to hold the invader and Gruffudd was killed. The united Wales was deliberately fragmented – divide and rule. Harold then married Ealdgyth, who thus had the unenviable fate of becoming widowed by battle twice in three years. But when William the Conqueror arrived in England he not only widowed Ealdgyth, he changed the nature of the Welsh relationship to the Saxons.

Prior to the Norman invasion the Saxon attitude towards the

Welsh was very much that of 'live and let live'. Occasionally there was a need, as the Saxon saw it, to teach the Welsh a lesson but Harold's invasion was an isolated and unhappy incident. The Norman Conqueror's attitude was different, however. William needed land with which to reward his followers and Wales was land; therefore he would call up the legal right to it and distribute it.

In fact the Normans did not have an easy time in their intended conquest of Wales. The country may not have had the unity bequeathed to it by Gruffudd ap Llywelyn – the constant civil wars saw to that – but first Rhys ap Tewdwr in south Wales and then Gruffudd ap Cynan in north Wales achieved a sufficient land base to thwart the Norman invader. In addition, Wales was not best suited to the Norman form of warfare with its emphasis on cavalry. Any invader of Wales needed quality infantry and, above all, the ability to consolidate gains because the Welsh could be very persistent resistance fighters.

Interestingly, William did not enter into a conquest of Wales as a policy decision: he wanted the land, but the commitment to conquest was lacking. Instead he chose to reward his followers by allowing them to do the invading for him. To achieve this he set up the Marcher lords, knights who owned land on the March – or border – between England and Wales. A lord of the March had a defined eastern border to his land, but the western border was his own affair. It was therefore the Marcher lords who pushed the Norman conquest into the Welsh heartland, becoming infamous for their treachery and their brutality. One lord 'slew the Welsh like sheep, conquered them, enslaved them and flayed them with nails of iron'. Not surprisingly the Marcher lords encountered the resistance of Gruffudd ap Cynan and Rhys ap Tewdwr. Their campaigns were local affairs: the families of Clare, de Braose and Mortimer pushing forward, building a castle, winning a skirmish here, losing one there. A remarkable side effect of this conquest by attrition was that the Normans were drawn into the Welsh style of tribal warfare, with small alliances being formed between Welsh princes – there were no kings now, except the one in London – and Norman lords, and even between the Norman king and the Welsh against one of the more powerful and belligerent lords. To cement these alliances there were numerous Norman-Welsh marriages and at times it appears that far from the Norman Marcher lords spreading westward, the Welsh were conquering eastward by the back door.

As might be expected, the timing of Norman conquests in Wales was dependent upon the terrain. In south Wales there are a large number of castles, indicative of frequent pushes and frequent successes. By the time Henry I died virtually the whole of south Wales, from Glamorgan to Pembroke, was in Norman hands. With Henry's death in 1135 however, Gruffudd ap Rhys and his son Yr Arglwydd Rhys re-established the kingdom of Deheubarth and pushed the Normans back towards the Severn. At the same time Owain Gwynedd, son of Gruffudd ap Cynan, pushed the invaders back to Chester, and Madog ap Maredudd and his brother re-established the kingdom of Powys. Things were not the same as before the arrival of the Normans, however. The century of occupation, partial or total, had caused certain areas of Wales to become pro-Norman, if not openly then certainly covertly. A good example is that of an early form of ethnic cleansing, with the Flemings of Pembrokeshire, who later rose with a spectacular lack of success against Owain Glyndŵr. This creation of enclaves of 'Englishness' in Wales was to have serious repercussions in later centuries.

Henry II attempted to subdue the new Welsh princedom but was not successful and had to accept the independence of both Owain Gwynedd and Yr Arglwydd Rhys – Lord of Ystrad Tywi, a Norman title despite its owner being Welsh. Owain died in 1170, Lord Rhys in 1187, Henry II in 1189. The deaths of Owain and Rhys caused internal strife in Wales, but Richard I was unable to take advantage of this because of his virtually continual absence on his crusades. King John came to the throne in 1199: by then Llywelyn ap Iorwerth – a grandson of Owain Gwynedd – had become Prince of Gwynedd. Llywelyn Fawr was an astute politician, and by good politics and the occasional exercise of a firm hand became the effective ruler of Wales by 1203. He strengthened his own position by marrying King John's daughter Joan, and by siding with the barons in the dispute with the crown which ended in the signing of Magna Carta.

Sadly the unity that Llywelyn achieved, and which was the only hope that Wales had against the ever-present pressure of the Marcher lords, was lost on his death. His son Dafydd lost control of Powys and Deheubarth and when Dafydd died his nephews Owain and Llywelyn, who succeeded him, saw their country so fragmented that when the Norman king invaded – finally using Welsh disunity to advantage – they could do nothing but accept the effective surrender of the Treaty of Woodstock in 1247. Wales was now just another group of lordships answerable to the English crown and, what was more significant, taxable by it.

When in 1255 Llywelyn ap Gruffudd, Llywelyn II, finally united Gwynedd, the fight that he led against the crown was little more than the rebellion of a Marcher lord. The Welsh, looking to re-establish their independence, did not see it that way, but that is how it appeared to the Norman kings Henry III and Edward I. At first Llywelyn restored to Wales those parts lost in the Treaty of Woodstock: he pushed back the Marcher lords to Cheshire, Shropshire and Herefordshire, retaking Brycheiniog (Breconshire) in mid-Wales. Significantly however, he failed to retake south Wales. By 1400 this area would have been in Norman hands for one hundred and fifty years. In 1267 the Treaty of Montgomery brought peace and Llywelyn became Prince of Wales. Had he stopped then he might have maintained all he had gained, but he continued to harass the borders of his country. While old Henry III was king he could hope to avoid crown retribution, but Edward I was different: he invaded

Wales, forcing Llywelyn to accept the Treaty of Aberconwy in 1277, which took back many of his gains. Llywelyn was quiet for a time, but then in 1282 rose again only to be killed in a skirmish at Cilmeri near Builth Wells. A huge monolith marks the spot where the last native Prince of Wales to be recognised as such was killed. Edward I built his 'ring of stone' castles, clamped like a manacle around Gwynedd and Wales, so that the people should always remember that they were a subject race.

The effect on the Welsh morale was catastrophic:

Oh God! That the sea might surge up to You, covering the land!
Why are we left to long-drawn weariness?
There is no refuge from the terrible Prison.

This was written by a bard in 1283, when not only was Llywelyn dead but also his brother Dafydd had been captured and barbarically executed. The independence known by the men of Gwynedd and Powys for almost a thousand years was over.

In one sense Edward's conquest was not catastrophic, as he was a humane man and left the Welsh with their language and culture. The problem was that the country was administered by those who felt that a subject race should know its place – downtrodden and well-taxed. The English never let the Welsh forget that they were Welsh. Eventually though, it came as a surprise to them that the Welsh still remembered.

When Edward gave the Welsh his son as Prince of Wales at Caernarfon in 1301, it was a well-meant gesture towards the new sycophantic class of Welsh gentry who were willing to accept the English king, and was favourably received by them, despite the bitter comment it now provokes. In Edward III's French wars the Welsh fought with distinction at Crécy and Poitiers, but at home there was always an undercurrent of resentment. There were frequent minor revolts and the harsh treatment these received only exacerbated the problem. The

Marcher lords continued to over-tax the native Welsh, in addition to treating them as serfs in their own country. From 1348 to 1350, the Black Death ravaged the land, adding to the torment. North Wales was a poor country agriculturally and the heavy burden of taxes and young men lost to war and disease meant that the Welsh slipped into a form of half-starved slavery for which, not unnaturally, they held the English responsible. The better farming areas of south Wales were able to survive more easily and therefore held less of a grudge. As the fourteenth century drew to a close, the Welsh of the north were as tinder waiting for a spark to ignite rebellion. The south was straw – whether it would prove to be dry or wet straw would depend on circumstances.

Owain Glyndŵr -
Not in the Roll of Common Men

Before 1400

...At my birth
The front of heaven was fully of fiery shapes;
The goats ran from the mountains, and the herds
Were Strangely clamorous to the frighted fields.
These signs have marked me extraordinary,
And all the courses of my life do show,
I am not in the roll of common men.

Though the words are Shakespeare's (from *Henry IV, Part One*), they are based on the Welsh legends surrounding the birth of Owain Glyndŵr. It was also said that on the night of his birth his father's horses were found in their stable, standing in blood up to their fetlocks, and that when Owain was still a baby in arms the sight of a sword or spear would start him shrieking, a shrieking which could only be silenced by his touching the weapon.

Such legends often grow up around the birth of famous men and in Owain's case very little that is factual is actually known of his early life – to such an extent that not even the date of his birth is established with any accuracy. He first enters history as a witness in a long-drawn-out case in the Chester courts: the case of Scrope v Grosvenor which concerned the right to a particular coat of arms. Since it lasted for nearly five years it must have been of tremendous importance to the contestants, an importance not readily understood in our age when heraldry, if it is considered at all, is viewed in the kindly light used to illuminate British eccentricity. In the late fourteenth century such was not the case, however, the right to arms being vital to any gentleman. On 3 September 1386 one who gave evidence was 'Oweyn Sire de Glendore de age XXVII ans et pluis'. One immediately obvious fact is that the entry in the court record is in French, still the language of the nobility. What we glean from the entry, apart from the difficulty which the clerk to the court experienced in producing a respectable representation of Welsh names, is that in 1386 Owain was twenty-seven 'et pluis'. The additional French phrase is awkward for anyone trying to pinpoint his date of birth. Its meaning is not dissimilar to 'over twenty-one', but it can also mean 'at least' since in those days age was not treated with the mixture of reverence and fear that we employ today. At the same trial Geoffrey Chaucer gave evidence, and he is listed as being 'forty et pluis', when good historical evidence suggests he was forty-six at the very least. It is difficult to believe that Owain just wanted to be 'over twenty-seven'. We can conclude that he was born probably in 1359, perhaps a few years earlier. From other evidence the dates 1349 and 1354 have been suggested: however, the earlier date seems to make him too old at the start of the rebellion and far too old at the finish, while the later date is to an extent discredited by the same source suggesting that Owain died when he was forty-six. Since it is thought he was alive in 1415, there is thus a contradiction.

Remarkably, in view of the position Owain now holds in the hierarchy of Welsh heroes, not only is the date of his birth unknown but also the place of his birth. It is widely assumed that he was born at one of the family's two Powys estates, but some stories have him born near St David's in the house of his aunt. Later in life, when Owain was looking for support from the whole of Wales for his claim to the princehood, his mother's descent from the royal house of Deheubarth was invaluable. The Pembrokeshire connection might have evolved then.

Owain's father, Gruffydd Fychan, died when Owain was still a boy. Gruffydd Fychan was descended from the royal house of Powys. He could also trace a line back to Rhodri Fawr, and since Rhodri was at the head of royal houses of Gwynedd, Powys and Deheubarth, Owain's lineage was a fine one. But it was to the

Powys house that Owain's family were closest and their holdings lay in 'Powys the bounteous and benign', as the greatest Welsh poet Dafydd ap Gwilym expressed it. Dafydd died in Owain's youth, but the beauty and energy of his poetry, his love of nature and his humour touched the bards who later sang the praises of Owain's family, estates and princehood.

In the Welsh of the day Owain was Owain ap Gruffydd, heir to the family estates at Glyndyfrdwy and Cynllaith. The first-mentioned of these is a name now taken by a hamlet beside the A5 road mid-way between Llangollen and Corwen, though the earlier name would have applied to a wider area. Glyndyfrdwy means 'the Gorge of the Waters of Dee'. The Dee, in Welsh Afon Dyfrdwy, is a beautiful river. Rising from the north-west tip of Llyn Tegid (near Bala) it cuts a channel between the high moorland of Y Berwyn to the south and that of Y Migneint to the north. At Corwen, after it has flowed north-east, the river turns sharply eastward towards Llangollen and England. Here, at first, it flows in a deep valley, a gorge defended at one end by Caer Drewyn and at the other by Castell Dinas Brân. This gorge formed the basis of Owain's local estates and gave him his name which, though variously rendered down through the ages, is now accepted as Glyndŵr. Within the valley Owain had a lodge, the remains of which – only a tree-topped conical mound – are still visible beside the A5 at (125 431), just under two miles (3.2km) west of Glyndyfrdwy hamlet. Today the shouts that predominate in the valley are from the canoeists who face the white waters of the Dee near Llangollen, though it is a sad irony that Owain's ghost, if it sat among the trees at the side of the old lodge, would have a very fine view of English invaders speeding along the A5 into the heart of Gwynedd.

The second of Owain's estates, Cynllaith, lay on the other side of Y Berwyn from Glyndyfrdwy, where the Cynllaith brook runs into Afon Tanat. Here, at Sycharth, Owain had his chief house for, although his name derived from the estate on the Dee, the farmland was better here. Perhaps too, in this lusher and more sheltered valley, life was easier and more relaxed.

Information on Owain's early life is scant and has to be inferred from snippets in chronicles of the time, from the songs of the bards and from knowledge of the general lifestyle of the sons of the nobility of that time. One chronicler tells us that Owain was sent 'to be an apprentice of the law at Westminster' – that is, sent to the Inns of Court in London, though this is not absolutely certain as no records exist for the Inns at that time. The immediate implication of this is that Owain was being raised in the manner of the *English* nobility and such is indeed the case. The Inns were not just the centre for anyone wishing to be trained as a lawyer, but acted as a public school for the sons of rich families, giving a good general education in the ways of government and of society.

Owain would have spent many years at the Inns of Court, perhaps as many as seven, and on leaving would have continued his education in the ways of the ruling elite by becoming a squire in one of the better houses of England, to tend to his lord particularly in battle and in tournaments and to learn how to be a soldier. Owain was squire to Richard Fitzalan, the Earl of Arundel, who appears to have taken the young heir under his wing when his father died. Almost certainly he was also squire to Henry Bolingbroke – King Richard's cousin and, later, Henry IV. If this was indeed true it was ironic that the close association of lord and squire should produce enemies at a later time. By then of course, the two had grown both up and apart: there may have been some personal animosity and Owain may have supported Richard as many Welshmen did – a policy unlikely to have endeared him to Bolingbroke.

We know something of the training that Owain would have received as a squire for, although no personal record of his service exists, there are contemporary accounts of the life of others. He would have run long distances and performed exercises in armour, to toughen him up, and would have practised long and hard with sword, mace and lance. But just as

26

we know little of any other part of his younger days, we cannot positively identify any campaign in which Owain took part. The Welsh bards – chiefly Iolo Goch – picture him in Richard's Scottish campaign of 1385. It is said that he cut a fine figure with his shining helmet sporting a scarlet flamingo feather: his lance shattered, but he used the jagged end to drive on Scots before him 'howling with fear like wild goats' in an attack so savage 'that no grass nor corn would grow in his tracks'. The same bards describe Owain at a tournament 'resplendent in gold and scarlet trappings of the finest kind' and 'shattering their bodies and overthrowing a hundred knights'. It seems likely that in true praise song fashion the bards overstated their case both for dramatic effect and to create the heroic leader that the people required. Certainly Richard did not honour Owain for his services in the Scottish campaign.

The last comment must not be seen to imply that Owain may not have had a distinguished military career. Detailed studies of his likely active service, in continental Europe as well as Scotland, suggest that he may have been a seasoned campaigner, and while probably guilty of embellishing the truth the bards were almost certainly not liars.

By 1398 Owain's military career was seemingly over. He was now about forty, perhaps forty-five, and had settled down to a quiet life at Sycharth. As a young man Owain had married Margaret Hanmer, daughter of Sir David Hanmer, a judge of King Richard's Bench and head of a rich and influential Flint-based family of Anglo-Welsh gentry. The bards who praised Owain loved her too: she was 'the best of wives' and 'of a knightly family, honourable, beneficent, noble'. The children of the marriage did not escape the same fulsome praise – they were 'a beautiful nest of chieftains'. If 'nest' the bard meant, then his thoughts at the time he penned the line were drifting towards pheasants rather than pigeons, because although the evidence on number and name is scant and sometimes contradictory, what is sure is that the Glyndŵrs had a great many children. Of sons, Gruffydd, Maredudd and Madog seem definite, but Thomas, John and David are also named. Of daughters there were many: Isabel, Elizabeth, Janet, Margaret, Catherine, Jane and Alice are named, though it may well be that Alice and Elizabeth are the same girl, or possible that Alice and Catherine were one and the same. Most sources suggest nine children, which certainly implies that Owain's wife Margaret was a strong, healthy woman. In late-fourteenth-century Britain, childbearing was a risky business.

The same bards who described Owain and his family, albeit with perhaps more enthusiasm than accuracy, also described Sycharth. It was a wooden house, which might be considered a strange construction at a time when the still-Norman English nobility were living in huge stone castles. Owain's position was different however, for though he was a noble with contacts in the English aristocracy, he was still a Welshman – a man from a subservient race. Barely a century had elapsed since King Edward's ring-of-stone had been tightened around the Welsh throat, and no Welsh noble was yet in a position to build in anything but timber, an inferior material.

Sycharth was protected by moats, and had nine rooms for guests, with linen as fine as any in London's Cheapside. Outside were fishponds and a dovecote, peacocks and a herd of fallow deer. The entertainment was luxurious and no one was turned away. Today all that remains of this most splendid of halls is a grassy bank, with the remnants of the moat still visible, standing beside a minor road that follows the Cynllaith stream southward from Llansilin, a hamlet six miles (10km) west of Oswestry.

To maintain his house, with its minstrels and bards and 'ale from Shrewsbury town', Owain had an income of around £200 per year which was more than adequate for the task. The income was derived from his estates and so it was doubly important to him when, in 1399, his neighbour Reginald Grey, Lord of Rhuthun, stole some land on the Glyndyfrdwy estate.

Owain was legally trained, he was a cultured man speaking Latin and French as well as English and Welsh. Despite his military background he chose to fight Grey in the courts. In the ordinary course of events he would have been successful. But times were not ordinary.

Richard II was a man of taste, but of expensive taste. Before he was old enough to hold the reins of power for himself, England had been governed by barons led by John of Gaunt, head of the house of Lancaster. Once Richard became old enough he offended these barons frequently, raised the exchequer levy on them and silenced their opposition by murder or exile. One to be exiled was his cousin Henry Bolingbroke, son of John of Gaunt. By 1399 Richard was all-powerful, but naïve enough to assume he could remain so despite his actions. He sailed for Ireland, to glory in the conquest of new lands and to extort more taxes. But as his ship pulled away from England, that of Henry Bolingbroke was heading towards it. Richard rushed back from Ireland, landing at Milford Haven and making for Conwy. Significantly, he had chosen Wales as his base. At Conwy he was met by Henry Percy, Earl of Northumberland, who persuaded him that Bolingbroke meant him no harm but wished only to re-inherit his father's land and title. Richard rode to meet Henry at Fflint Castle, but was ambushed and captured. He 'willingly' abdicated in favour of Henry, retired to Pontefract Castle in Yorkshire and was never seen again.

At Conwy the royal baggage train was captured by Henry's followers, but the Welsh, recognising the treason of Henry's actions, 'liberated' the baggage and its wealth of silver and gems. Later most of the baggage was recovered, but Henry was not interested in 'later', he wanted it now. Richard had been pro-Welsh and the Welsh liked him, for all his faults – though it has to be admitted that his pre-Ireland tax rises had been unpopular and they had not rushed to join him as he travelled from Milford Haven to Conwy. The Welsh also had the royal baggage, and, for, both these reasons, Henry IV was not well disposed towards them.

Following Glyndŵr's rebellion, there was a persistent story in Wales that at one time he had been a squire to King Richard. It has even been suggested that he may have gone to Ireland with the king and been at Conwy when he met Northumberland. The latter could be true even if Owain had not gone to Ireland, for it would have been no great effort to travel from Sycharth to Conwy and if he was there he would have been seen by Northumberland. Owain was a fine figure of a man, very tall and wearing his hair long, down to his shoulders, at a time when the norm was hair close-cropped for ease of wearing a helmet.

In the circumstances, Owain stood little chance with his lawsuit in the English Parliament: the barons of the new king had as little time for the Welsh as had Henry himself. The Bishop of St Asaph exhorted the king and Parliament to be wary of creating new enemies before the ripples of the change of order had died away, but to no avail. Owain's case was not only dismissed – bad enough in itself – but with the comment: 'What care we for barefoot Welsh dogs.' For a proud man of royal blood, it was a humiliating experience. And one not to be forgotten.

1400

In Wales, all was not well. Richard's army disbanded into Wales, some of the soldiers sickened by the way Bolingbroke had deceived their king and usurped his throne. Others were just at odds with the world, in the way that old campaigners can be. Talk that Richard had been murdered made the anger seethe even more, and rumours that he was alive and a prisoner made them long for justice. When Henry IV again raised the taxes, the temperature of a hard-pressed nation, continually goaded at its border and treated with contempt by Englishmen everywhere, began to rise.

The Constable of Harlech wrote to the Chamberlain of Caernarfon, who in turn wrote to the king, that Welsh rebels were in touch with Scots from the 'Owt yles' (the outer isles) and that these were to land at Abermaw (Barmouth) to help the men of Meirionnydd rise. The Meirionnydd men were stealing horses and acquiring weapons: there were 'recheles men of divers countries' in wild Wales waiting to foment rebellion. Lord Grey of Rhuthun was noticing similar murmurings in the northern Marches, and was anxious to be given greater powers to root out the troublemakers and deal with them. Strong measures were required, Grey noted, 'else trewly hitt will be an unruly Cuntrie within short time'. But King Henry had other problems on his mind. The time was ripe for the even more unruly Scots to be taught another lesson, for which he was raising an army for the teaching. He told his officers in Wales to offer pardons to anyone who had defied the law, in the hope that the dissatisfaction would die away.

Lord Grey was particularly bothered by the activities of Gruffydd ap Dafydd, a local bandit who had the temerity to steal the lord's horses. At the king's order Gruffydd was offered a pardon and a position as a master forester, provided he gave himself up at Oswestry. He did so, and was lucky to escape alive. For many men the experience would have been a salutary lesson in dealing with the authorities, but Gruffydd was aggrieved enough to confront Grey with his treachery in a letter. After a straightforward statement of the Oswestry betrayal he writes: 'I was told that you are in purpose to let your men burn and slay in any land which succours me and in which I am taken. Without doubt as many men as you slay for my sake and as many houses as you burn for my sake as many will I burn and slay for yours. And doubt not that I will have bread and ale of the best that is in your Lordship.'

It is a bold threat and earnestly meant, despite the

gentlemanly close to the letter where Gruffydd ended, 'But God keep your worshipful estate in prosperity'!

Grey's face colour must have matched his name when he read the letter, but in fact it was ammunition in his battle to increase his holding on the March. He sent a copy to the Prince of Wales, Henry of Monmouth – later to become Henry V of Agincourt – together with a copy of his reply to Gruffydd in which he promised the Welshman, 'But we hoepe we shall do thee a pryve thyng; a roope, a ladder, and a ryng, heigh on gallowes for to henge. And thus shall be your endyng.'

It was a poetic ending and Grey must have felt the Fates were on his side alone when they offered him Owain Glyndŵr. Henry IV was raising his army for Scotland in the time-honoured fashion of calling for each noble to bring his quota of men to the standard. Reginald Grey as chief Marcher lord was given the task of passing on the summons to the local nobles. Owain would have been an asset to Henry, as a proven fighting man with a knowledge of Scotland and the Scots. His absence from the army so soon after Parliament had ruled against him would have been badly taken. Grey knew that, and somehow the summons was not passed on.

King Henry marched without Owain. His army was humiliated, a fact hardly likely to improve his temper, and he gave leave to Grey to move against the treacherous Welshman. A butt was needed for the royal anger and Owain would be that butt. Grey knew that a straightforward attack would be unlikely to capture the Welshman, who would escape long before troops arrived, and that a show of force might provoke hostility in his followers. He therefore arranged a meeting, ostensibly to discuss Owain's problems: the latter agreed, but limited the number of men to accompany Grey. Grey arrived ostensibly with the small band stipulated, but a second group secreted itself near the house to await a signal to attack. Legend has it that Iolo Goch saw the ambush and, as he entertained hosts and guests with a bardic poem, he told Owain of the planned attack in cryptic verse. Owain left the room and escaped the house. The long, luxurious autumn of his life at Sycharth was over.

On 16 September 1400 Owain was at Glyndyfrdwy, the estate protected by the gorge of the Dee and its look-outs. With him were his brother Tudur, from whom he could be distinguished only by a wart under his left eye, other members of his family and some close associates. A standard was raised – the red dragon of Wales – and Owain was proclaimed Prince of Wales. A poet there sang:

> Cambria's princely Eagle, hail,
> Of Gruffydd Fychan's noble blood,
> Thy high renown shall never fail,
> Owain Glyndŵr, great and good,
> Lord of Dyfrdwy's fertile Vale,
> Warlike high born Owain, hail!

In London four bells at the corners of a saintly shrine in Westminster rang of their own accord, not once but four times - a knell for the English king? And in Wales the stream at Cilmeri where the severed head of Llywelyn ap Gruffudd had been washed, ran red all day. Blood, but whose?

Not unnaturally Owain decided to strike his first blow for Welsh independence against Grey at Rhuthun. But if it is easy to see why Grey and Rhuthun, it is less clear why he struck at all. What decided this dignified and cultured man to become a rebel at an age when most men of his time were content with heroic memories?

It is probable that, at Glyndyfrdwy, Owain received envoys from many Welsh families, pouring out their hatred for the Marcher lords and the English king. The generations of physical, emotional and economic suffering at the hands of the English had been polarised by the action of Henry IV against the pro-Welsh Richard, and by the contempt of Henry's Parliament for Owain, their highest-born. A French knight at Henry's court said at the time of the investiture of young Prince Henry as Prince of Wales, that if the new prince were to have Wales he must conquer it, 'for in my opinion the Welsh would on no account allow him to be their lord, for the sorrow, evil and disgrace which the English, together with his father, had brought on King Richard'. Everyone but Henry and most of his lords failed to read the signs: those like Grey who did read them played local, petty politics with the anger they betrayed.

The bards were spreading the word that freedom was at hand, that a hero had arisen. Owain was carried on the tide, perhaps. He must also have been looking for the restoration of his Sycharth estates, though a man need not be a prince to regain his land. Owain must have known that to take Sycharth was one thing but to hold it would be quite another, and that the holding might require the creation of a free Wales.

On 18 September, Owain's first army rode into Rhuthun. The town was preparing for its fair, with stalls laid out and crowds gathering. The motley band of men that came through the town's gates were armed not only with swords and bows, but with sickles and rough-cut spears. In the shadow of Reginald Grey's red castle they fired the town and looted the market: the damage was estimated at £1,400, perhaps £350,000 in present-day terms. None of the townsfolk were killed, but fourteen rebels were captured and Grey hanged them all.

Owain's band moved quickly. By 24 September they had fired and looted Dinbych (Denbigh), Fflint, Hawarden, Holt, Rhuddlan and were advancing on Welshpool. But in the six days since the sacking of Rhuthun, Hugh Burnell, Sheriff of Shrewsbury, had raised a small force from Shropshire, Staffordshire and Warwickshire and had marched to Welshpool. On the banks of the Afon Efyrnwy Owain's band was routed, the men disappearing back to the valleys whence they had come.

The next day Henry and his army arrived in Shrewsbury. There he executed Goronwy ap Tudur, a kinsman of the

Anglesey Tudurs, a formidable family who had fought with King Richard. Goronwy's death was intended, in Voltaire's famous phrase, to 'encourage the others'. Goronwy's dismembered body was sent to Chester and Hereford, Ludlow and Bristol to encourage them even more.

The local rebellion had ended with the Efyrnwy defeat and the arrival of the royal army, but a second rebellion broke out in Ynys Môn led by Rhys and Gwilym Tudur, cousins of Owain. To quell it swiftly, Henry marched immediately to the island. All along the route the Welsh submitted to the king's army, but at Rhos Fawr near Beaumaris there was a sharp exchange with a band of Rhys Tudur's men. The Welsh retreated, then Henry burned and looted the Franciscan house of Llanfaes Abbey before retreating in turn. He had sacked the house because the friars openly supported the rebels, but also because the Abbey land was rich, the loot paying his mercenary soldiers.

Henry marched south through Gwynedd. He reached Mawddwy on 13 October, then turned east and arrived back in Shrewsbury on the fifteenth. The country was peaceful. He offered a pardon to the leaders of the revolt, and Tudur Glyndŵr surrendered. But Owain was excepted from the pardon, his confiscated lands being given to John Beaufort, Earl of Somerset. The rebellion, it seemed, was over.

1401

In excepting Owain from the general pardon Henry IV made a mistake, but that was inevitable as he had placed himself in a no-win position. If he pardoned Owain and returned his lands to him not only would he declare openly his inability to police Wales but would also publicly humiliate Reginald Grey who had started the whole episode, though he would placate Owain and, in the short term, the Welsh. If, instead, he confiscated Owain's land, he would please Grey – though not as much as if he gave the land to him – and the English, but would antagonise

Owain and, probably, the Welsh. Henry took a calculated risk: it might have paid off, but he ensured it would not by allowing the English Parliament to enact a set of laws which were bound to evoke not antagonism but hatred in the Welsh.

It is not easy to understand why the Normans bothered the Welsh. The Saxons had pushed them back into their upland country and built Offa's Dyke at the point where they had decided to halt. Early Norman conquests had been for land and for glory, but the mineral wealth of Wales was not apparent a thousand years ago and there was little glory in pursuing the warlike and hardy Welsh into their hills where they could hide easily, appearing only to harass the invader and always cloaked in the vile mountain weather. It seems the Marcher lords - who, by law, were allowed to take any land they could hold - found the 'Welsh dogs' an easy source of self-aggrandisement, sport and loot. Small wonder the English Parliament was contemptuous, and equally small wonder that the Welsh were angry.

In early 1401 the contemptuous Parliament decided that no Welsh person could hold official office, or marry an English man or woman. The Welsh could not live in England and must pay for the damage done to English property in the rebellion of 1400. Owain was still at Glyndyfrdwy, for although technically the estate had been confiscated it would have been a brave man who tried to enter the tight Dee valley and claim the land. But Gwynedd had accepted the royal pardon and Owain was isolated. By March 1401 he may well have had as few as seven followers, with a few retainers. The situation was not good and without the new laws Owain might have sunk into obscurity. The savage legislation broke open the old wounds, however, though not there at Glyndyfrdwy, but at Conwy.

On Good Friday the commander of Conwy Castle, John Massy, marched his garrison to church outside the castle walls. The castle, still one of the finest medieval buildings in Britain and a tribute to its builders, an almost perfect war machine, was left in the care of just two guards. Massy was an Englishman, well versed in the way of European war. War in the early fifteenth century was a game played by kings and lords, moving their armies of peasants and mercenaries like chess pieces on the board of Europe. Like all good games there were rules, invented by the nobles and the church to avoid unholy behaviour, at least towards each other and not on Sunday. The Ynys Môn brothers, Gwilym and Rhys ap Tudur, were not bothered by these noblemen's rules. With the garrison gone, two Welshmen approached the castle gate disguised as carpenters, to carry out jobs inside. The two-man guard opened the gate to them and were killed immediately. Gwilym ap Tudur and forty of his men then fired Conwy and escaped into the castle.

By the time Massy had grasped what was going on the town was burning beyond control, thousands of pounds' worth of damage had been done to English merchant property and the rebels were in control of the castle. Massy called the Chief Justice of North Wales to Conwy. The Chief Justice was Henry Percy, a man of thirty-five, the same age as the king, christened Hotspur by the Scots when he fought them on his sixteenth birthday. Hotspur was the son of the Earl of Northumberland who had helped give Henry the crown, and was a favourite of the king. Knowing that Wales was a tinderbox and that Conwy could be the spark, he was anxious that the castle should be retaken quickly and wrote to the king asking for leave to offer a pardon to the rebels if they surrendered. There was no real alternative, for Conwy was so sound a fortress that only a long siege could hope to retake it if negotiations failed. The Tudurs accepted the terms, but King Henry did not. Again he could not win – to pardon the rebels would be to admit that no town in Wales was safe, but to lay siege would allow Wales to realise his impotence. He decided not to sanction the pardons.

Negotiations dragged on for weeks. The Tudurs could not hope to survive as there was no Welsh army large enough to relieve the castle from its blockade. Eventually nine of the rebels were taken by the others, bound and given over to the English in exchange for free passage for the remainder. Before Gwilym and the rest of his men were back in Ynys Môn, the nine had been drawn, hanged, disembowelled and quartered. Their butchered remains were sent about the country as a visible sign of the king's ruthless intentions towards all rebels. Exchanging hostages was a common occurrence, as is apparent in many cases in this war. It was not, however, usual even in a time of treachery and murder, for hostages to be butchered as so many chickens, and then scattered all over the country. Whatever was said during the negotiations, the Welsh contingent were mistaken to trust an enemy who wanted to set an example. Whatever the Welsh hoped to achieve in handing over hostages, Henry Percy's subsequent actions were despicable

What had been gained by this act? It is certain that the Tudors were acting independently of Owain, though their cause was similar. Excited by Owain's achievements they had joined in, perhaps not realising the dire position in which they might be left as a result of this run up a blind alley. They can hardly have had much desire for rebellion after the appalling aftermath to their act. For Hotspur the end must have been equally unsatisfactory. True he was a soldier and medieval warfare was a nasty business, but Hotspur was not a barbarian and butchering the nine rebels, while expedient, can have given him no satisfaction. Certainly by the end of May Hotspur was disillusioned about his position and about activities in Wales. In letters to Henry he complains of lack of funds to pay his army and of his intention – unless things improved – of returning home. In reality he had no quarrel with the king over cash, but was rather unhappy with Henry and, perhaps, unhappy with his treatment of Wales. Later Hotspur was to claim that he only wanted to help Henry regain the Lancaster lands, not to usurp Richard's crown. Later, too, he was to sign a treaty with Owain and in 1401 may even had had contact with the new Prince of Wales. Conwy may therefore have been more of a victory than it seemed, however squalid.

As the spring of 1401 replaced the winter of 1400, the Welsh warmed gently to their new prince. At Oxford, always a favourite university with the Welsh, there were demonstrations in support of Welsh nationalism and many students returned home to fight for freedom. In England the Franciscans and many nobles, convinced that the Welsh revolt would return Richard to the throne, gave money to the cause. As much as £500,000 flowed across the border, though at some cost in human lives. One William Clark had his tongue pulled out for daring to speak against Henry, had his right hand cut off for daring to write against the king and was then beheaded, the final punishment certainly nullifying the effect of the other two but being, so the English thought, poetically savage. William Clark was not alone in his sacrifice.

By early May, with Conwy Castle still occupied, Owain had collected some men together, though he was unfortunate when Hotspur encountered a group of them while he was showing the flag near Cadair Idris. Owain's small band was routed and, though the loss was hardly significant, he decided to move his summer operations to south Wales.

Owain needed a mountain lair to which he could return and chose a secluded valley on the northern slopes of Pumlumon. There, near land that now lies beneath the waters of the Nant-y-Moch reservoir, he raised his standard. A stone cairn and plaque now record the event. It was a symbolic gesture although the initial response was not overwhelming, the first army being just a few hundred strong. The band raided south and east, stealing food and cattle and burning houses: Llandrindod Wells, New Radnor and Montgomery were looted and fired.

But strangest of all, the abbey at Cwm-hir was attacked. Beneath the turf of the abbey grounds the headless body of Llywelyn the Last lay interred and the abbey was a shrine to nationalism. But the Cistercian monks were believed to be in league with the English. It was the second time it had been razed, the first time having been by an English king who suspected the monks of Welsh sympathies. It is likely that the true sympathy of the attackers in each case appears to have been with the abbey treasury: war is not only a nasty, but an expensive business.

Welshpool was attacked again, but resisted stoutly and Owain's men withdrew to Pumlumon. There in the Hyddgen valley they rested, apparently unaware that an army was on the move towards them.

In south-east Wales there was a large body of immigrant Flemings, brought over by Henry I to boost the local woollen and craft industries. In time they had spread out, moving northwards and even occupying parts of southern Ceredigion. In doing so they had displaced and antagonised the inhabitants Welsh. Any unruly behaviour among the natives could cost the Flemings dearly so they decided to take matters into their own hands and collected an army of fifteen hundred to march north.

At Hyddgen – either because of excellent planning or appallingly slack defence by the Welsh, they succeeded in surrounding Owain with his band of about four hundred men. The Flemings had superiority in numbers, they had the element of surprise in their favour and the benefit of the terrain as they poured downhill into the valley and on to the trapped Welshmen. The Flemings should have won but, as a contemporary account notes, 'they hemmed him (Glyndŵr) in on all sides so that he could not possibly get off without fighting at a great disadvantage. He and his men fought manfully a great while, in their own defence, against them. Finding themselves surrounded and hard put to, they resolved at length to make their way through or perish in the attempt: so, falling on furiously, with courage whetted with despair they put the enemy, after a sharp dispute, to confusion; and they pursued so eagerly their advantage, that they bade them give ground, and in the end to fly outright, leaving two hundred of their men dead on the spot of the engagement'.

It was the first real battle of the war, not only won by the Welsh, but in such a resounding way that loyal countrymen everywhere were cheered by the news and anxious to join the rebellion. To mark the battle site two dazzling white calcite blocks were placed in the Hyddgen valley. The blocks were the Covenant Stones of Owain Glyndŵr, named for a pilgrimage.

In June Hotspur pulled his army out of north Wales and returned to Northumberland, and from then until September Owain's men ravaged the whole of Wales killing, burning and looting. The lands of the English were, as expected, the prime target, but not all the Welsh were in sympathy with the rebellion. Those who were not found to their cost the price to be paid for failing to be enthused.

All summer King Henry waited, though why is not at all certain, but finally – when it seemed possible that Owain might actually invade England – he moved and on 8 October an English army arrived at Bangor. It marched to Caernarfon and turned south. The weather was excellent, the opposition non-existent, and the king soon reached Ystrad Fflur or Strata Florida, an abbey south-east of Aberystwyth. The house was Cistercian, a brother abbey to Cwm-hir which had been destroyed because the order was said to be pro-English. But at Strata Florida, King Henry's English army decided that the Cistercians were actually pro-Welsh: the abbey was looted, its holy vessels stolen and many monks were murdered. Henry ordered that his knights' horses should be tethered at the high altar with inevitable consequences for the church. His knights drank the abbey's wine cellars dry in a two-day drunken spree, then smashed down the buildings and fired the ruins.

Henry moved on towards Llanymddyfri (Llandovery) where a local squire, Llywelyn ap Gruffudd Fychan, promised to lead the army to Owain's hideout. For several days the squire led Henry about, until it became obvious that he was wasting their time and energy. Challenged, he admitted he had sons with Glyndŵr and was leading the army astray. Llywelyn was butchered in Llanymddyfri square while King Henry watched. And in case such medicine might be good for the natives, other similar doses were meted out as the army fruitlessly sought its prey in mid-Wales. Owain's men made occasional forays to pick off outriders, or to raid a baggage train, but would be away before any of Henry's main force arrived. The guerrilla tactics were successful, but costly in civilian lives and livelihoods. Since the English could not batter the Welsh army they battered the Welsh countryside.

Henry strengthened the garrison in the southern castles, feeling that in so doing he had subdued the area. In truth an Englishman was safe now only within his massive stone walls, and to make the point clearly Owain attacked Caernarfon in November and Harlech in December. Neither attack was successful – indeed the Caernarfon attack cost many lives – nor was it likely to be, but it had the desired effect of keeping English heads down.

But despite his successes Owain knew that he had little real chance against the English unless he could gain more support. He might have the majority of the Welsh on his side, but Henry had the professional army and the castles. In an effort to obtain more support Owain wrote to Scotland and Ireland, noting their common ancestry and the prophecies which told that, with their help, Owain would rid the countryside for good of their 'mortal enemies, the Saxons'. The letters, written in French, are in the convoluted form of the time, but clearly written by a man capable of pinpointing the likely features that would best draw support from cousin Celts. They are also notable for the form and frequency of the address to the King of Scotland – 'redoubted lord and Sovereign Cousin', and the King of Ireland – 'dread lord and most trusty Cousin'. Owain was not only a fine general, but an astute politician.

He was certainly astute enough to hedge his bet on the likelihood of gaining support and total victory. Through the Northumberland Percys he entered into a peace negotiation with Henry. The king was inclined to accept: Owain wanted only the return of his estates and a pardon for himself and this time it would not be unreasonable to accede. Henry was hard pressed in Wales and peace at any cost might be better than having to continue fighting and, probably, to continue failing to protect the English in Wales. A nice face-saving withdrawal on both sides seemed to suit everyone. But it did not suit Grey, who hated Glyndŵr, or Beaufort, who wanted Glyndŵr's estates. In the end it was decided to use peace talks as a means of capturing Owain, but to his great credit Percy would have none of this.

So the die was cast. Since Henry would not be allowed to make peace, he and Owain would have to make war. It was probably a decision that both men feared and regretted. By the end of 1401, a year that had started so badly for Owain seemed to be ending well, but it is doubtful whether Owain was thrilled with the prospects for 1402.

1402

In February a comet crossed the sky, 'a terror to the world', and a cause of some excitement and much outright fear in the superstitious peasant classes of Europe. The poets saw the comet as a sign. Such a fiery star had been seen when Arthur had been born, and there had also been one above Bethlehem. The portent was clear – Owain was warrior-king and saviour. As if to prove the point the comet, when seen from England, pointed towards Wales, and on occasions curled its tail and took on the shape of a dragon.

England and Wales were struck by violent thunderstorms, lightning tearing the sky apart. At one English church lightning struck the roof and half demolished the building. The terrified congregation had no time to escape before the Devil came in, dressed as a Franciscan monk, one of the order who sided with

Owain. He jumped over the altar and fled, passing so close to one man that the man's legs were blackened for all time, as if from fire. The smell of sulphur took everyone's breath.

As if to prove the omens correct – though who would deny them in any event? – as the comet was heading into the Welsh sky Owain captured his greatest enemy, Reginald Grey. It seems that, on 31 January, Owain appeared before Rhuthun, challenging Grey to a fight. Then, or so one story has it, Owain shod his horses backwards so that Grey believed his cavalry had retreated. Grey charged the few remaining infantry only to discover that they were merely helmets set on top of poles. Too late he realised his mistake, as the Welsh poured out from woodland on his flanks to hack his men to pieces. Other stories suggest that Grey's own men had betrayed him, through love either of Owain or of the bribe he offered them. Either way the day ended with the Lord of Rhuthun, trussed up and obscene with anger, being taken to a makeshift prison either at Llansanffraid in Powys, or in Snowdonia. No one man can ever be held responsible for a war that lasts half a generation: there must be others who help him, knowingly or by stupidity in default. But the revolt of Owain Glyndŵr was started by Reginald Grey, and it is likely that it continued beyond the winter of 1401 because of his efforts to ensure it was prolonged. His capture was a poetic justice.

Grey was immediately ransomed. Though Owain had cause to hate this man who had sought to humiliate him and had actually stolen his lands and made him an outlaw, butchery was out of the question. Grey was worth a lot of money. To be exact he was worth £10,000, the bulk to be paid in one month with Grey to then be replaced by his son who would stand surety for the rest. In fact the colossal sum took months to produce, and its collection ruined Grey financially as his lands were sold to raise some of the cash. He had started the war to make a financial killing: he ended it in penury. Moreover, whereas by his actions he would like to have seen Glyndŵr dead, he survived only by

Owain's clemency and had to sign an agreement never to raise a sword against him again.

But though the omens and the capture of Grey raised Welsh morale, and convinced many that Owain was indeed Freedom reborn, there were others who were unconvinced. Owain's cousin, Hywel Sele of Nannau near Dolgellau, might not have been convinced of the correctness of the revolt. What is certain is that he also had a long running dispute with his relative, which might explain his actions when, in an attempt to smooth things over, the Abbot of Cymer Abbey, near Nannau, persuaded the two men to meet. They walked on Hywel's estate with Hywel carrying his bow. When a deer was started, Hywel fitted an arrow – aiming and firing not at the deer but at Owain, whose life was saved because he was wearing a mail coat below his jerkin. Hywel was never seen again, but forty years later a great oak split and inside its hollow centre was found the skeleton of a man. Owain had killed Hywel and concealed his body in *ceubren yr ellyll*, the hollow tree of a fiend. The troubled spirit of Hywel haunted the area, and the Haunted Oak was shunned until it was destroyed by lightning four hundred years later.

Elsewhere in Wales Owain had little to fear. True the great castles were still in English hands, but castles were a strange war engine. In our days of enhanced mobility it is difficult to understand how a castle could be of any use. True it protected its inhabitants very well, but why not just walk around it? Or sit outside and wait for the garrison to die of starvation? The truth is that the castles' worth can only be understood in the context of medieval warfare, when to keep a huge army in the field was a prodigious logistical feat. The supply lines had to be maintained – leave a castle untaken and as you moved on its garrison came out behind you to chop off your umbilical cord. Sit around it – and the cost of doing nothing could mean insolvency.

But in 1402 Wales was largely Owain's; he had no supply

lines to protect, he had all the time in the world. The castles were symbolic of a power that had retreated from the fray. In England King Henry was closing his mind to the Welsh problem. He had not won the crown merely to fiddle about with the Scots, Irish and Welsh: he wanted a crusade to win him glory and everlasting salvation. It was a fine dream, but one about to be rudely shattered.

In spring and early summer Owain devastated English north Wales. Significantly he left Dinbych, Hotspur's estate, alone and moved southward towards Powys. By June he was approaching the land of the Mortimers. Edmund Mortimer was uncle of the Earl of March who, as direct descendant of Edward III and the named heir of Richard II, had a greater claim on the English throne than the usurper Henry. The existence of the young earl was of concern to Henry who obviously did not feel strong enough to dispose of him, but wanted him well-guarded in case he became the focus of anti-Lancastrian feelings. Edmund, the boy's protector, mustered an army of several thousand and marched to meet the Welsh.

At Pilleth (Pyllalai) a hamlet near Knighton, Owain's men at long last stood their ground on the ridge of the steep slope of Bryn Glas – next to the present beautiful church, not in the valley as sited by the Ordnance Survey. Surely, Edmund dared not attack up the slope, for that would have been ludicrous. But that is what he ordered his men to do. His Herefordshire-levied troops with English knights in support charged, and as they did Mortimer's Welsh archers poured arrows into them, apparently in an act of spontaneous support for Owain. The English army – to be precise, the English part of Mortimer's army – was slaughtered.

When it was all over, and it would not have taken long, the Welsh stayed on their ridge above the huge pile of dead. Estimates vary, but there were probably between one and two thousand men stretched out on the slopes. Owain's men were accompanied by what was for those times the normal entourage of women – camp-followers, wives, cooks and so on. It has been written that, 'After the batayle ful shamefully the Walsch women cutte of mennes membris and put hm in here mouthis.'

And: 'The shameful villainy used by the Welsh women towards the dead carcasses was such as honest ears would be ashamed to hear and continent tongues to speak thereof. The dead bodies might not be buried without great sums of money being given for liberty to convey them away.'

And again: 'A thousand... butchered; upon whose dead corpses there was much misuse, such beastly shameless transformation by those Welshwomen done as may not be without much shame retold or spoken of.'

To put it another way the English dead were mutilated and then the bodies were sold to the grieving relatives. Many were, apparently, not claimed and only a century ago a farmer ploughing Bryn Glas uncovered the heaped bones. They were re-interred and a clump of fir trees planted on the spot. Today these trees stand tall against hill and sky.

The stories of the aftermath of the battle may have been exaggerated: propaganda is not a new weapon. In addition, not one of the above records was written before 1530, generations after the date of the Battle of Bryn Glas. But there is probably a grain of truth. Owain's campaigns had been bloody, but then the times were bloody – the English had invented the 'scorched earth' policy in France to frighten the natives into submission, and to reduce their will and ability to fight back. At Pilleth the pent-up hatred of a century of effective slavery might have been vented in one vile outrage.

But what is the true story of the Bryn Glas battle? Later writers have made much of the tactics employed by Rhys Gethin, Owain's lieutenant, in taking up a position beyond the ridge and so effectively ambushing from behind the hill, a very advanced technique. But if Rhys was so good, why was Bryn Glas so rare as a pitched battle? There were probably only four thousand Welsh there, but Henry's armies apart, that was a considerable force in Wales during the revolt. And what of the Welsh archers changing sides?

King Henry thought he knew the answer and accused Mortimer – himself captured in the fight – of treason. Later events do suggest that Mortimer was anti-Henry and he did become surprisingly pro-Glyndwr in a short space of time. And, of course, Hotspur was his brother-in-law. Owain demanded a ransom for Mortimer which Henry refused to pay. Hotspur was furious: how could the king help pay for Grey and refuse to pay for Mortimer? A chronicler of the time reports a face-to-face confrontation, with Henry touching his sword and Hotspur shouting, 'Not here, but on the field of battle.' And Hotspur returned to Northumberland.

With Mortimer's men destroyed, Owain swept south destroying Abergavenny and Cardiff and sacking the bishop's palace beside Llandaff Cathedral. He also maintained his blockade on Caernarfon and Harlech castles, and now besieged Cricieth.

King Henry was troubled. Four thousand Scots were massing on the northern border and he could not count on Hotspur. He needed a quick victory in Wales or his kingdom could well be in ruins by the year's end. In late August he massed a hundred thousand men on the Welsh border, in three separate armies, and in early September he invaded Wales.

For several years the bards had been telling the people that Owain was supernatural. Now, with a vast army in their country, the people needed a sign and Owain needed to show his ability at 'calling spirits from the vasty deep'. As Henry's three armies advanced, the weather changed and for fourteen successive days the rain, driven sometimes by fierce winds, lashed down on his men. The rivers rose and became impassable. The men had no shelter and slept in chilling rain. The supplies were destroyed by water. Henry's tent was thrown down by a storm and he survived only because he was still in armour. In mid-September the armies retreated with men dying of exposure along the roads back to England. The invasion was over, no sight or sound of Owain had been seen. All was hidden behind his magician's cloak of weather!

The English soldiers – without hot food for days, chilled and sodden wet, frightened by the storms and by the knowledge that unseen Welshmen were picking off stragglers – knew now that Owain could command the elements. 'Through art magicke as was thought, he [Owain] caused much foul weather of windes, tempests, rain, snow and hail to be raised for the annoyance of the King's army, the like of which had never been seen.'

Shakespeare in Henry IV, Part One has Owain saying:

Three times hath Henry Bolingbroke made head
Against my power. Thrice from the banks of Wye
And sandy-bottomed Severn have I sent
Him bootless home, and weather beaten back.

And he had a stone that a raven had spat out for him, which made him invisible. How could anyone fight such a man?

1403

Towards the end of 1402 two events, widely separated in space if not in time, gave heart to both sides. In Wales Edmund Mortimer married Owain's daughter, Jane, thus ensuring a pact between the Welsh prince and a possible English king, the Earl of March. Edmund wrote to his estate manager:

I greet you much and make known to you that Oweyn [sic] Glyndŵr has raised a quarrel of which the object is, if King Richard be alive, to restore him to his crown; and if not that, my honoured nephew, who is the right heir to the said crown shall be king of England, and that the said Oweyn will assert his right in Wales. And I, seeing and considering that the said quarrel is good and reasonable, have consented to join in it, and to aid and maintain it, and by the grace of God to a good end, amen.

But in the north, at Homildon, Hotspur defeated the Scottish army: he captured its leader, the Earl of Douglas, and freed King Henry from immediate fears of invasion.

The allegiance with a possible new English king was good, but before Owain could consider or assist in invading England, he had first to secure Wales. South-west Wales, the land of the Flemings – still smarting from the Hyddgen defeat – had to be taken. To that end Owain campaigned south and west, though he still maintained the siege of the northern castles. Letters written by the constables of Dinefwr and Brecon castles, who were brothers, allow us a first-hand glimpse of conditions at the time. They talk of Owain with eight thousand lances at his back, dominating the area with his feared lieutenants – Rhys Gethin, Rhys Ddu and Rhys the son of Llywelyn from Llanymddyfri who had died for misleading the royal army. From Dinefwr comes: 'There is great peril for me for they have made a vow that they will all have us ded therin; wherefor I pray thee that thou wilt not boggle us, but send to us a warning within a short time whether we schule have any help or no.'

The king too, was made aware of these cries for help. From Brecon came:
...to ordain thereupon speedy remedy for the destruction and resistance of the rebels in those parts of South Wales, who are treacherously raised against you and your Majesty, so that your castles and towns and the faithful men in them be not thus ruined and destroyed for lack of aid and succour. And besides, may it please your lordship to know that the rebels...are lying near the town of Brecon doing all the mischief they can to its town and neighbourhood, and they purpose, all of them together, to burn all pertaining to the English in the same parts if they be not resisted in haste.'

The message from Hereford:'...the whole country is lost unless you go there as quick as possible. Be pleased to set forth with all your power and march by night as well as by day, for the salvation of those parts.'

It is clear that in every part of Wales Owain's men were in command outside the castle walls. But he did not have it all his own way. In early July Owain halted his thrust into the Fleming land of Pembrokeshire at Laugharne, later to become a place of pilgrimage for those seeking a Welsh poet. He wanted to talk to Lord Thomas Carew, who held the castle there. Several local castles had fallen easily: Owain was hoping for another, and probably feared a direct fight with the Flemings who were difficult adversaries, despite their poor showing at Hyddgen. As talks progressed a band of Welshmen slipped quietly around the side of the castle, taking a hillside route to avoid detection. But Carew was a wily foe and his men, set in the hills in readiness for just such a move, ambushed the band of seven hundred men. Not one escaped.

To make things worse a local seer, Hopkin ap Thomas, told Owain that he would be captured and dragged away beneath a black banner, on the Gower. Owain had set great store by the bardic prophecies on his behalf and while it is idle to discuss whether he actually believed it all, it is obvious from the fact that he consulted the seer that he would have to take heed of his advice. Some have suggested that Hopkin made his prophecy in order to protect the Gower. Whether that is true or not Owain retreated from the area and back towards Caerfyrddin (Carmarthen).

While his thrust into south-west Wales was being halted by the defeat at Laugharne, news was arriving of the destruction of his estates at Sycharth and Glyndyfrdwy. The attacks were undoubtedly upsetting for Owain, though he may have consoled himself with the knowledge that he was now acting out his life on a wider stage. What was of greater significance, though it could hardly have been realised at the time, was that the leader of the English force was the English Prince of Wales, Henry (of the cry 'God for Harry, England and St George!' at Agincourt). Agincourt would be won by a leader trained in the rugged terrain of Wales. Now he was just a boy, but he was a good learner as time would tell.

While Owain was stopped at Laugharne, King Henry was raising an army in England. He had received the letters from Wales begging him to help the beleaguered fortresses, and others from his son saying that the retainers in the northern Marches were deserting for lack of pay. It would be natural therefore to assume that he was preparing an invasion of Wales. Such an assumption would be quite wrong. In fact Henry was preparing to invade Scotland!

At this remove in time it is difficult to comprehend the almost blind recklessness of such a move. To the west the Welsh were threatening to invade England, while the Scots occupied a country filled with a people both poor and consumed with hate for their southern neighbours. It is likely that even as Henry was preparing his Scottish army, news reached him that was to have a direct bearing on the outcome of Owain's rebellion, even though it concerned only Englishmen in England. Following the Homildon battle Hotspur ransomed his prisoners, including the Earl of Douglas, after the time-honoured fashion. Such high-born captives were spoils of war. But Henry demanded the prisoners – and thus by implication the ransom – for himself. For Hotspur this was the last straw. First Mortimer had been refused ransom and now Henry wanted his prisoners. Having already had talks with Owain and Edmund Mortimer, the Percys decided to break with the king. The old Earl of Northumberland was ill but Hotspur, eager as always to be on the move, departed immediately towards Wales. At Chester he formed an army, mostly untrained but with troops of the now-friendly Earl of Douglas – glad just to be allowed to kill Englishmen! – and the Chester longbowmen, feared everywhere.

On 20 July Hotspur's army approached Shrewsbury. To his horror the town was occupied not by a small royal garrison or – much better (and expected?) – by Owain's men, but by the king, who had shown an absolute mastery in the art of forming and force-marching an army. Thirty thousand troops were waiting for Hotspur's fifteen thousand men. and to add to Hotspur's misery, he discovered that the hamlet where he had to spend the night was called Berwick. Long ago a seer had told him he would die in Berwick and he had assumed this would be in a border war with the Scots: now he saw it was to be in civil war with the English king. In despair he said 'I perceive my plough is now drawing to its last furrow.'

Despite the despair, on 21 July at a site now called Battlefield, 3 miles (5 kms) north-east of Shrewsbury centre, Hotspur commanded with his usual flair. His Chester archers slaughtered the king's bowmen and created havoc in the ranks of his knights. Only when Douglas, inflamed by the sight of all those Englishmen in disarray, charged, nullifying the archers' effect, did the tide turn. The fifteen-year-old Henry of Monmouth turned Hotspur's flank, receiving a face wound for his efforts. Confusion reigned, but when it cleared Hotspur himself was dead, his army defeated.

They buried Hotspur close to the field, along with at least four thousand of his friends and foes. Henry had his body dug up and exhibited in Shrewsbury market-place. Not again would yearning for a live hero be allowed through mere shortage of a dead body. For good measure the body was quartered and distributed: the head went to a spike on York town gates. A church was built over the mass grave, the only church in England that is a war memorial.

Had Hotspur won then, history would have been so different as to be beyond computing. Had he reached Owain then Wales would have won its freedom – at least until Mortimer or Northumberland chose otherwise. So why was Owain not at Shrewsbury? Henry called him a coward, and a tale arose that Owain watched the slaughter from an oak tree, afraid of pitched battles. That is unlikely. It is more likely that Hotspur's impetuosity cost him and Owain victory, that and poor communications. If Hotspur had awaited his father's better health he would have had a bigger force and given Owain time to extricate himself from the problems at Laugharne. Even had he not waited, had word reached Owain in time he might have made it to the field.

But two things are clear. The first is that Hotspur underestimated the king's logistical ability and his son's fighting qualities. The second is that the Welsh were betrayed by the nature of their campaign. Had Shrewsbury been taken and held, then the battle would have gone to the allies. The strike-and-run guerrilla warfare was winning battles, but it was not winning the war.

From Shrewsbury the king marched north to quell an incipient rising in Northumberland. The old earl, sick and sorrowful, rode through York's gates with his king, past the blackening head of his son, and came to heel.

In Wales Owain continued to cut a swathe across the land, apparently oblivious of Shrewsbury and its implication. He invaded Herefordshire, dragging legislation out of Henry that any Welshman found in any border town would be executed. The situation for the beleaguered English worsened and on 15 September Henry invaded Wales for the fourth time. He marched to Caerfyrddin (Carmarthen), issuing orders, proclamations and pardons without number. He then turned and marched out again. It had taken four days and achieved nothing. No rebels were seen, let alone engaged, and within a day or two of his departure from Wales, Owain was in Glamorgan taking Cardiff, Caerffili, Newport, Usk and Caerleon.

Owain now had at least ten thousand men at arms, perhaps as many as thirty thousand and, in addition, he was receiving some small assistance from the French. Chiefly this involved piracy on the southern English coast, actions guaranteed to keep English soldiers out of Wales, but there was a landing of troops in Caerfyrddin and Breton soldiers were assisting at the siege of Caernarfon.

Ignoring Shrewsbury as being an English affair, it had been a good year for the Welsh. Optimism ran high as winter brought 1403 to an end.

1404

In early 1404 Owain was so secure in Wales that he could concentrate his efforts on the remaining strongholds, the castles of north Wales. The records that are preserved show just how impregnable the great castles were when defended by able and courageous men – but conversely just how useless they were, except as symbols, if they were not being utilised by a marauding army. At Caernarfon twenty-eight men were holding the castle against the combined efforts of Owain and his small squadron of French allies. To visit Caernarfon castle now, with its museum and well-tended lawns, and the hustle of visitors, is to be impressed by the scale and immense beauty of the structure. In January 1404 just twenty-eight men kept watch from those towers and battlements, forever fearful of another attempt to scale their walls. Henry IV had forgotten them. They watched, hour after hour, ticking off the hours to when they would die of starvation if Owain did not reach them first. That is true bravery, not the valorous act of desperate men in the alien situation of battle, but the day-long, night-long courage of men in a normal, yet extraordinarily abnormal, situation.

At Harlech south of Caernarfon, perched on a rock outcrop between the sea of Cardigan Bay and the unremitting rocks of the Rhinogau, the men broke. Owain badly wanted one of these great castles and, it is thought by offering bribes or pardons to the beleaguered garrison, he won Harlech. When the gates were finally opened to the Welsh there were sixteen men left. Of all the castles this was the one which raised Welsh hearts: it was here that Bran the Blessed had had his rocky fortress and the site was Welsh back to pre-history.

Harlech was no Sycharth: it was harsh and cold where Sycharth had been lush and friendly. But to the castle Owain brought his family, and if it did not suit his wife and children, it enraptured the poets. A Welsh Prince of Wales, and at an ancestral place!

> Here is the life I've sighted for long
> Abashed is now the Saxon throng
> And Britons have a British Lord
> Whose emblem is the conquering sword...

The poet extolled Owain, the hero of the watery dell, the bloody spear in field. The spear would be bloodier yet, but who could deny an old poet what he had waited a lifetime to see?

> Grace, wisdom, valour, all are thine,
> Owain Glyndowerdy divine,
> Meet emblem of a two-edged sword,
> Dreaded in war, in peace adored.

> Loud fame has told thy gallant deeds,
> In every word a Saxon bleeds,
> Terror and flight together came,
> Obedient to thy mighty name;
> Death in the van with ample stride
> Hew'd thee a passage deep and wide...

In the wake of Harlech, Cricieth and Aberystwyth fell and now Owain was in control of Wales from coast to coast. So secure was his position that he could stop being solely a warrior king and start to be a statesman. He called a parliament at

Machynlleth, a convenient spot to gather together 'few persons of sufficient consequence' from every cantref of ancient Wales. Today the site of this first Welsh parliament house holds an ancient, though not sufficiently ancient, dour stone building with a simple inscription.

The parliament was a regal occasion, but again death was in the van. Dafydd ap Llywelyn ap Hywel, known as Dafydd Gam – 'gam' from crooked, because he had squint-eyes – came from Brecon. He was red-haired and long-armed, a man of quick temper who had fled Brecon at a young age after killing a neighbour. At Machynlleth he tried to kill Owain, probably as a service for Henry Bolingbroke whom he had known from childhood, for when he fled Brecon he joined the service of John of Gaunt.

Gam's plot was discovered but surprisingly, in view of the treatment Hywel Sele had received, Owain did not kill him. This has often been ascribed to Gam's being a relative, but that is not the case. It was another Gam who was a relative – and Hywel Sele was in any case a cousin. The reason for the clemency is not known, although another theory is that such an act might have been made to project Owain as a magnanimous ruler. Equally it might have been to ensure that Gam rotted away nastily in a damp dungeon somewhere. In fact Gam was eventually released and fought and died for Bolingbroke's son at Agincourt. He was knighted as he died, winning fame for his often quoted reply when his king asked, before the battle, how many French there were: 'Enough to kill, to take prisoner and to run away'. He is widely believed to have been the model for Fluellen, Shakespeare's all-encompassing Welshman – though that name is clearly an English attempt to spell Llywelyn. It is an irony that this Welshman of all of them should be so honoured.

But though he did not kill Gam, Owain destroyed his estates at Brecon. It is said that the cultured Owain even lapsed into verse over the incident, telling Gam's bailiff:

Canst thou a little red man descry,
Looking around for his dwelling fair?
Tell him it under the bank doth lie,
And its brow the mark of a coal doth bear.

At Machynlleth Owain may have been crowned again. Certainly he took a royal coat of arms though, significantly, it was not the lion of Powys, despite his descent from that line, but the four lions of Gwynedd, the ancient warrior kingdom. There were representatives from France and Spain at Machynlleth and gifts were brought for the new ruler. He appointed a Chancellor, Gruffydd Young, and sent him and his brother-in-law John Hanmer to France to negotiate a formal treaty of allegiance.

Not everyone was impressed by this show of government and Adam of Usk wrote with typical Norman sentiments: 'Owen and his hill-men...held or counterfeited or made pretence of holding parliaments.' But despite Adam another parliament followed at Dolgellau and Owain's forces moved towards the English border. The French treaty was signed at Aberystwyth and the French prepared a fleet to sail to Wales. In its ships would be an army for the invasion of England.

Owain's forces again ravaged Herefordshire, but once more stopped at the border. The panic over probable invasion was now such that beacon fires were prepared to signal its occurrence and Prince Henry of Monmouth wrote in great alarm to his 'most dread and sovereign lord and father'. The plea fell on deaf ears, King Henry did nothing either to reinforce or relieve the beleaguered castles of north Wales, or to bolster the defences of the Marches.

Richard Beauchamp, the young Earl of Warwick, was less complacent – or more probably less hard-pressed financially – and decided that the Severn was as far as he wanted Owain to advance. In June he crossed the river with a large force, in search of the small army that had now turned south toward Glamorgan. At Campstone Hill, about 3 miles (5 kms) south-west of Grosmont Castle, Beauchamp found his quarry and there was a fierce battle in which Owain's standard was captured. Remarkably Owain himself was almost captured – what was he doing here so close to the English border, so far from Harlech? We shall soon see.

The defeat was a bitter turn of events, for it suggested again that the Welsh were no match for a disciplined English army. Perhaps sensing that the result could damage Welsh morale, Owain re-grouped and pursued the English who unwisely had not chased the Welsh after they broke at Campstone. At Craig-y-Dorth, about 3 miles (5 kms) south-east of Monmouth, he caught them, beat them soundly in a running battle and, to make the point, chased them back to Monmouth town.

In August Owain was in Cardiff. In fact his decision to be there was the reason why he was so nearly captured at Campstone, and why he had therefore been available to restore Welsh pride at Monmouth. The reason for his presence at Cardiff lay in the English Channel, for that month a fleet of sixty vessels had sailed from Harfleur to land an army in Wales for the invasion of England. The fleet was under the Count of March, and every day Welsh soldiers lined the Glamorgan coast waiting for it to appear over the horizon. They waited in vain. Whether by orders or on his own (non-) initiative, the count sailed up and down the English channel pretending to be an invasion fleet. He succeeded in frightening the south coast towns, but he failed to frighten Henry IV who ignored him as he ignored Owain. This time the king was proved right. Owain's men became sore-eyed in vain. In November the Count returned his fleet to Harfleur: he had not landed any troops anywhere.

By November Owain too had retreated, back to his castle stronghold at Harlech. Despite the lack of real activity in the showy procession of the Count of March's fleet, the treaty with the French was ratified. In addition several treaties were made with English border provinces. Edward de Charleton, the Lord of Powys, made a truce from his Red Castle, at a cost of course. And so did the people of Shropshire. Theirs was the more important treaty, for it guaranteed their peace – again at a price – for three months, not from rebels to the English crown but from the 'Land of Wales'.

1405

Early in 1405 there was a plot to release the young Earl of March, the true heir to the English throne, from the benign – for the moment – but steady grip of King Henry. Some authorities claim that the Tri-partite Indenture signed between Northumberland, Mortimer and Owain was drawn up at this time, and that the plot was necessary for the treaty, the signatories needing a figure-head for their cause. In general however it is believed that the treaty was signed in 1406 and that the plot was an independent scheme – and it is that sequence that is followed here.

The young earl and his brother were at Windsor for the Christmas of 1404, in the charge of Lady Despencer, while the king and his court were elsewhere. A small party including Lady Despencer and the boys left Windsor as the new year dawned, and made haste westward. It was required only that they crossed the Severn, for once in Wales there was no hope for the survival of any pursuing band. It is believed that Henry heard of the escape while the party was still in Berkshire and a desperate chase began. The earl's party reached the border of Gloucestershire. The safety of the Severn was only a day away now – but it was one day too far, as they were caught by Henry's men.

Lady Despencer, in fear of her life, claimed her action was part of her brother's plot to kill the king, and also told the name of the locksmith who had made her the keys she had used for the escape. Her brother, the Duke of York, denied the charge, and was eventually pardoned. The locksmith had his hands cut off. Such was the justice of medieval England.

Whether this abortive rescue mission occurred before or after the signing of the Tri-partite Indenture, it was another blow to Welsh hopes though again, as after Shrewsbury, Owain's men continued as before. Rhys Gethin, that loyal lieutenant, collected an army of eight thousand men and moved into Monmouthshire. Again there were fears that England was to be invaded, and Prince Henry decided to make a stand. Throughout the years of Welsh dominance the young prince, still only eighteen, had steadfastly refused to ignore the Welsh rebellion. Now, it seems, he had decided that even if his father was happy with the situation west of the Severn, he was not. At Grosmont Castle he collected a small army and waited.

Rhys arrived at Grosmont and burnt it to the ground. But Welsh joy was shortlived, for Prince Henry emerged from the castle and forced them to stand and fight. After the battle the prince wrote to his father:

My most redoubted and most Sovereign lord and father...your people gained the field, and vanquished all the said rebels, and slew of them by fair account in field, by the time of their return from the pursuit, some say eight hundred, others a thousand, being questioned upon pain of death.

The engagement had been a disaster for the Welsh. There were Welsh archers on Prince Henry's side and they remained loyal, inflicting terrible damage on the army of Rhys. Owain was greatly concerned by the defeat and immediately sent his brother Tudur to regroup the local forces. Owain's son, Gruffydd, arrived to join Tudur and they prepared to attack the castle at Usk to which Prince Henry had moved. The Abbot of Llantarnam Abbey celebrated a mass for the soldiers, who were told that those who died bravely would that night 'sup in

61

heaven'. There were men who would find out if he was correct.

The Welsh attacked the castle and Prince Henry again opened the gates and charged out, breaking the Welsh ranks and scattering the army in confusion. The Welsh fled east to Mynydd Pwll Melyn, less than 2 miles (3 kms) from Usk. There Tudor and Gruffydd attempted to form a battle-line, but Prince Henry was a new enemy. He did not fight and wait, he fought and chased. The Welsh lines were not complete before the prince arrived to break them. The Welsh ran into the woods – called Coed y Pwll-Llyn by the Ordnance Survey in an ugly misrendering of Welsh – and were relentlessly pursued, hacked down or captured. Tudur Glyndŵr was killed and jubilation ran through the English until the lack of a wart under the left eye showed he was not Owain. The Abbot of Llantarnam was also dead as were many, many more. Gruffydd, roped to his captive men, was led back to Usk where, to encourage the men of south Wales, three hundred prisoners were beheaded. Gruffydd was spared, if being imprisoned in the Tower is being spared. In appalling conditions he survived six years, dying eventually of disease.

Adam of Usk wrote of this battle in his home town, where the English nobles 'slew with fire and the edge of the sword many of them without ceasing'. Gruffydd, he noted, was 'cut off by pestilence'.

The remnants of the shattered army edged back towards north Wales. When one soldier asked another abbot who had helped at the mass before Usk why he had not stayed to sup in heaven, the abbot replied that it was one of his fast days.

In the wake of Grosmont and Usk, King Henry, shrewd as ever, offered pardon to all who renounced the rebellion and virtually the whole of south-east Wales responded to his call. Realising that the time had come to reinforce the Welsh change of heart by advancing into mid- or north Wales, Henry gathered an army of forty thousand men on the border at Hereford. To add to Owain's problems the safe island of Anglesey was lost when Beaumaris Castle was retaken by the crown. The situation looked desperate: it was clear that a summer invasion of mid-Wales would inevitably lead to more defections to Henry, and equally clear that after the reverses at Grosmont and Usk, Owain's army could not hope to stand and fight. What Owain needed was time, and to obtain that he required a diversion.

Whether by happy chance, or by chance assisted by his own councillors in Northumberland, the north of England now rose in revolt under Richard Scrope, Archbishop of York. As usual Henry saw any other rebellion as being more serious than that in Wales, and immediately moved his army northward. At Shipton Moor in Yorkshire the revolt was put down and Scrope was captured and butchered, but also executed was one of Owain's ambassadors to Northumberland. It is still not clear whether Owain fuelled the rebellion, or whether the north saw the chance to rise because Henry was pre-occupied in Wales.

Henry stayed through the summer maintaining the peace in the north, and Owain used the time well, allowing his battered men time to recover, strengthening the morale of the wavering parts of his principality and then, in late July, gathering ten thousand men in Pembrokeshire to await another French invasion fleet. The French put to sea with one hundred and forty ships, but this time the weather would not allow them to parade in the channel. To the unrelieved joy of the Welsh the seas drove the French, not homeward, but to Milford Haven. The French army disembarked, together with its leader Robert of the One Eye, but with none of its horses all of which had died of thirst on the crossing.

Estimates of the size of the French force vary, but it was probably around five thousand in total. They joined Owain's army and the combined force marched on Haverfordwest, which was razed. The castle was not taken, and to express their displeasure the Welsh slaughtered the citizens of this English and Fleming township. Next, Tenby received the same treatment. At this stage it appears that the French would like to have gone home. However, an English fleet under Lord Berkeley arrived, sinking many ships at anchor - the French were marooned. That many pressed men are needed to replace one volunteer is proverbial, and with his mixture of both Owain marched on Caerfyrddin. The town surrendered and next Glamorgan was punished for accepting the royal pardon. Owain was again in control of Wales.

Now, for the first and only time, in mid-August 1405, Owain invaded England. It was three and a half centuries since England had last been invaded by a foreign power in numbers sufficient to cause alarm. King Henry, despite his war-weariness after five years of endless struggle, and his near-bankruptcy, hurried to Worcester to face the invaders who were camped on nearby Woodbury Hill. The chosen camp site was indicative of Owain's indecision at this time. It was a beautiful defensive position, but what had he to defend? He could hope neither to conquer England from a defensive camp, nor to feed his men indefinitely here in hostile England. But Owain feared pitched battles with the English, which may have been his reason for staying at Woodbury. If that was the case he would have been better retreating, for it can have done little for the Welsh and French morale to sit it out day after day staring at the superior English army. There were skirmishes, a few hundred soldiers died and then Owain retreated. Not since the Norman invasion had a French army sat in England, but the French, like the Welsh, would not do so again.

King Henry followed the retreating army, but it was not an easy pursuit. Owain's scorched earth policy worked and Henry's army was forced to disengage, starving. Henry regrouped at Hereford and invaded Wales for the fifth time, his intention being to stop the French from regaining their ships. He might have succeeded, but the Welsh winter turned on him again. The rivers filled, making the fords impassable. Some said that Owain conjured the storms for one final time against his old foe. Henry turned home in frustration and in October crossed from Wales to England yet again: but this was to be the last time.

In Wales the French managed to reach their ships and went home, although some French soldiers stayed behind to enjoy the cold rain and snow of a Welsh winter. They were homesick and miserable and they took it out on their host's lands and property. By the spring of 1406 when they too departed, Wales was glad to be rid of them.

1406

The year opened badly for Owain. Providence delivered the heir to the throne of Scotland into Henry's hands when King Robert's son James was captured en route to France. With such a hostage, Henry immediately secured his northern border.

It is to this time, early 1406, that the Tri-partite Indenture between Northumberland, Mortimer and Owain is assigned. Whether it was actually signed now, or had already been signed in 1405 is largely academic however, for the treaty was never much more than a scrap of paper. The three men promised each other every possible assistance – short of actual help.

What indeed had they to offer? Old Percy had fled to Scotland where the Scots, reluctantly accepting the necessity to be polite to Henry while he held their prince, offered to exchange him for the Earl of Douglas, held since Shrewsbury. Northumberland therefore fled the country, landing in Wales at Aberdaron in early 1406. He brought nothing but his name, though that might have been useful in fomenting rebellion in the north. All Mortimer had to offer was his nephew, the Earl of March, and he was in King Henry's hands. But Owain still had Wales.

The treaty was signed on 28 February, in either 1405 or 1406 – the latter date supported by the presence of all three men in Wales at that time. It is interesting as a historical document, particularly in the defining of the borders of the three new estates which would comprise England and Wales. It begins: 'In the first place that these lords, Owyn, the Earl and Edmund shall be mutually joined, confederated, united and bound by the band of true league and true friendship and sure and good union.' Which of them, one wonders, believed that in those treacherous times there was any more clamorous noise than a hollow ring to these words?

As if fearful of just such treachery, there is a long section on the need to be 'good and faithful friends' and the requirement of 'good faith'. To reinforce this second section a short third section is a résumé of it, labouring again the point that there should be mutual respect – 'Each of them, also, shall be content with that portion of the kingdom aforesaid, limited as below, without further exaction or superiority.'

The apportioning gave Northumberland England north and Mortimer England south of a line very roughly joining Kidderminster and Lowestoft. It is the border of Wales that holds the interest however. Owain will have:

> the whole of Cambria or Wales, by the borders, limits and boundaries under-written, divided from Loegira, which is commonly called England; namely from the Severn Sea as the river Severn leads from the sea, going down to the north gate of the city of Worcester; and from that gate straight to the Ash tree, commonly called in the Cambrian or Welsh language Owen Margion, which grows on the highway from Bridgnorth to Kynvar [Kinver] thence by the highway direct, which is usually called the old or ancient way, to the head or source of the river Trent; hence to the head or source of the river Merse [Mersey]; hence as that river leads to the sea.

The treaty ends not with a restating of the need for friendship or good faith, but with a decision that should two of the parties fight, the third shall act as 'good and faithful counsel' whose decision on the quarrel would be final. It is clearly a document drawn up not by true friends but by fearful, suspicious allies brought together by a cause bigger than anything they could survive alone.

The use of the ash tree boundary marker was a necessity to Owain's bards, allowing them to spread the word that an ancient prophecy of Merlin was to be fulfilled. They cursed Henry, the 'mouldwharp cursed of God's own mouth'. A dragon, a wolf and a lion would come, their tails entwined. The Thames would be choked with corpses, England's rivers would run with blood and beneath the blood would drown the mouldwharp Henry.

Owain must have been aware that the treaty was largely worthless while his two co-signatories were in Wales with him, rather than in England preparing for the fight. Certainly, rather than rely on the help they could not hope to offer in the short term at least, Owain decided to renew overtures to the French. In early 1406 another parliament was held, probably again at Machynlleth, and from Pennal, a hamlet on the other side of the Dyfi, Owain wrote to Charles VI of France on 31 March.

In the letter Owain is quick to seize on the religious rift in Europe, the Papal Schism, which had caused a rival Pope to be enthroned at Avignon. Owain promises that in his new country the Archbishop of St David's and all bishops will be appointed by France's Benedict XIII and not the Roman Gregory VII. At this point in the letter Owain includes a paragraph which makes a true statesman of the writer irrespective of the cant that precedes it and the hypocrisy that follows. He asks for permission to 'have two universities or places of general study, namely one in north Wales and the other in south Wales, in cities, towns or places to be hereafter decided and determined by our nuncios and ambassadors for that purpose'. Had Owain been successful in his struggle with the English, this far-sighted request would have given Wales its colleges before the Scots had theirs. It is to Owain's credit that even as he was struggling to maintain a free Wales, he could conceive of the need to plan for an educated generation of Welshmen.

After the call for universities Owain comes to the point of his letter. Henry the usurper is accused of burning down churches and cathedrals and of slaughtering Welsh clergy and monks. King Charles is called on to sanction a crusade against Henry, for in addition to these sins against Holy Orders he is also a follower of the Roman Pope. The Owain who wrote these comments on Henry was, of course, the man in whose name Abbey Cwmhir, St Asaph and a good number of other holy houses had been laid waste. War is a terrible thing, making hypocrites of the greatest of men.

The letter to Francis is signed, 'Owenus Dei Gratia princeps Walliae' and is dated in the 'sixth [year] of our reign'. Charles VI was delighted with Owain's letter and sent greetings and gifts – but he did not send an army.

As 1406 drew on, King Henry became ill, stricken with a disease which wasted his body and his mind. It may have been leprosy or syphilis, but whatever it was it left Prince Henry with a freer hand. He formed that free hand into a fist and prepared to punch Wales. On St George's Day, Prince Henry was campaigning in Wales. Somewhere – history does not record exactly where – he met a force of Welshmen and killed a thousand of them. Another of Owain's sons died in this battle.

Prince Henry campaigned all over south Wales, for to leave Owain in the north would be to leave him free but isolated. Much of the country reverted to the king. The prince demanded heavy fines for perceived mis-deeds, and the landowners paid readily. The alternative was probably bleak, but the irony was that south Wales' money now helped the English crown fight, while the north Wales country, ravaged continuously for so many years, could no longer sustain Owain's cause.

Owain still occupied the castles of Aberystwyth and Harlech, and on this Cardigan Bay coast he still held a regal court: one story has him exercising the royal prerogative of pardon over a felon. There are, in addition, many tales of Owain wandering the country, sometimes alone, sometimes with just a few followers. These stories are curious. Though as the days shortened to the end of 1406, it was becoming clear that the Welsh were facing an uphill struggle just to survive, Owain still held sway over two-thirds of Wales. But the tales are persistent. They have him living in a cave at the mouth of Afon Dysynni, not far south of Harlech, and in another cave on the side of Moel Hebog in Snowdonia. There is a story in an old manuscript that he was a guest of Sir Lawrence Berkrolles at his Coity castle. Sir Lawrence was an English knight and was reputedly struck dumb – literally, not just by the shock of the moment – when Owain shook his hand as he was leaving and revealed himself.

It would be easy to dismiss these stories, or to assume that they are misplaced in time from a period several years later when Owain really was on the run in Wales, but it is to this period that the following verses are said to relate:

> I saw with aching heart
> The golden dream depart;
> His glorious image in my mind,
> Was all that Owain left behind.
> Wild with despair and woebegone
> Thy faithful bard is left alone,
> To sigh, to weep, to groan.
>
> Thy sweet remembrance ever dear,
> Thy name still ushered by a tear,
> My inward anguish speak;
> How could'st thou, cruel Owain, go
> And leave the bitter tears to flow
> Down Gruffydd's furrowed cheek?

What was happening at this time? While it is true that Owain may well have had a price on his head, why should he have been wandering the countryside when his family has securely sheltered in Harlech castle? No satisfactory explanation can be given. Never again was Owain to be a threat, and indeed it is very difficult to actually catch sight of the Welsh prince from early 1406 onwards. Had the horror of the war and its failure taken away the reason of his cultured mind, leaving him a wandering, old, weary and confused man, or a man who for his own safety had to be escorted about in secret, so that his still-faithful followers could use his name to strike terror into their enemies?

Had he decided that he would return to his origins as the magical leader of the Welsh, and thus sought refuge in a cave to sleep out the years until he should come again?

Is it possible, even, that he was already dead... killed, murdered or worn out? No evidence from the remaining years of the revolt ever satisfactorily explained his death or where he was buried.

1407 AND AFTER

The remaining revolt was no glorious last stand on some bloodstained Gwynedd field. It died of starvation from lack of funds and men, and from the strangulation of the English Prince of Wales, Henry of Monmouth.

Prince Henry decided that Aberystwyth and Harlech, the castles that were still held by Owain, should be captured. With no firm base the Welsh could not hope to defend the country against the prince's combination of savagery and pardons – the stick and the carrot.

In the summer of 1407 Prince Henry besieged the old castle of Aberystwyth, beautifully set beside the sea. By an irony of fate, beside the ruins of the castle there now stands a college of the University of Wales. But in 1407 what stood there were two cannon, the newest weapon in the royal armoury. The castle garrison, used to the old-fashioned siege engines some of which were also present, must have looked at these new machines with curiosity, though doubtless their wonder did not survive the first bombardment.

Seven cannon were brought in all, including the king's 'gonne', a four-and-a-half-ton monster, and the 'Messenger'. With them came five hundredweight of powder, nearly nine hundredweight of saltpetre and three hundredweight of sulphur. The cannon pounded the walls of the castle, terrifying the garrison. But the cannoniers were also terrified, one of the 'gonnes' bursting during the siege and killing everyone close to it.

The siege continued until mid-September when Owain's castle commander, Rhys Ddu, offered Prince Henry a curious compromise whereby there would be a truce until 24 October, when fighting would recommence. If by 1 November the castle had not been relieved, then the garrison would surrender. A treaty to that effect was agreed and Prince Henry removed his men to Strata Florida before returning to England. There he received the grateful thanks of Parliament. As he did so, Owain reinforced the castle and cancelled the treaty.

The winter of 1407–8 was one of the worst for many years: raw, pitiless wind and bitter cold, with the whole land under a carpet of snow from Christmas until March. To add to the Welsh misery late in 1407 the Duke of Orleans, their champion at the French king's court, was murdered in France. In the wake of the killing, England and France signed a truce. Now the English crown was free of threats from both Scotland and France. Then in early 1408 the old Earl of Northumberland attempted one last uprising and was killed at the battle of Branham Moor. What few hopes the Welsh may have had as 1407 came to an end, died in the freezing start to 1408.

There were some minor revolts when the summer sun had removed the snows from the land of Wales and strangely these were in Glamorgan, the first area to have accepted the royal pardon. The heavy fines imposed by the crown caused ill-feeling and this was played upon by the northern rebels. But it was too late for the men of Glamorgan to find that the devil they did not know was no better than the one they knew. The rebels were ousted and the heavy hand of England strengthened its grip. In the north the castles of Aberystwyth and Harlech were again under siege and with no relief possible from land or sea the constant bombardment of Prince Henry's forces eventually broke the spirit of the defenders. Late in 1408 Aberystwyth fell, and then in 1409 Harlech, the last redoubt, surrendered.

Within Harlech's walls Edmund Mortimer had died, and at its surrender Owain's wife and the last of his children were taken. Chivalry prevailed at last however and Owain's family were taken unharmed to London. Later, it is believed, Margaret Glyndŵr returned to Wales to live out her life with one of her daughters. For the rest the Welsh were treated with surprising leniency, Prince Henry having astutely noted that the pardon worked better than the sword. There were other brief skirmishes in later years, but never the decisive final defeat that signalled an end to the revolt. Perhaps the true end came after a raid on the Shropshire border in 1410, when from the Red Castle at Welshpool a band of English emerged to crush the raiding party. Rhys Ddu and Rhys ap Tudur were taken prisoner, as was Philip Scudamore, an Owain sympathiser from Herefordshire. After the custom of the day, following the inevitable executions the head of Scudamore was spiked at Shrewsbury, that of Rhys Ddu at Chester and that of Rhys ap Tudur at London. Along the border and in England's capital, the blackening heads of his last generals told of Owain's defeat.

Of Owain himself nothing certain is known from about 1406 and nothing at all from 1412. Prince Henry of Monmouth succeeded his father and became Henry V on 21 March 1413. In July 1415 the new king offered a pardon to Owain and any of his men who remained free. There was no reply. In February 1416 the king tried again, using Owain's son Maredudd as an intermediary. This certainly implies that Owain was still alive, though Maredudd may not have known this for certain when he accepted his assignment. This new offer was not taken up either, though Maredudd himself did accept a pardon in 1417. By then Owain would have been at least fifty-eight years old – no great age by our standards, but we do not expose ourselves to years of chronic weather and the worries of war.

Perhaps Owain was dead. Certainly the poets thought so:

and when thy evening sun is set,
may grateful Cambria ne'er forget,
Its morning rays, but on thy tomb,
May never-fading laurels bloom.

There were some who believed that Owain went to live with his daughter Alice and her husband John Scudamore in Herefordshire's Golden Valley. There are several versions of this story. One has Owain taking the living of Kentchurch church and dying there: the priest Sion (John) of Kentchurch was a poet and had a reputation as a mystic. There is a fifteenth-century painting of the priest in Kentchurch Court, showing an old, weary man with sunken, staring eyes. Another version has Owain dying at Monnington Court, a mile or two northward. It would be a sad irony if either of these places held his body, for each is in England and but a short distance from Grosmont Castle, whence Prince Henry of Monmouth emerged one day in 1405 to sign the death warrant of the revolt with a crushing victory.

Confusion was added to the story of Owain's death when it was announced that his grave had been found at Monnington. But not Monnington Court – Monnington-on-Wye, northward yet again. The confusion arose because of the similarity of name and this is often quoted. One author from early this century not only maintained that the Wye village was Owain's resting place, but gave the date of his death as 20 September 1415!

There were others who maintained he did not die in the

peace of his daughter's house, but lonely, cold and weary on an exposed ridge in Gwynedd, or in the woods of Glamorgan.

The bards depicted him sleeping with his men in some concealed cave, awaiting the time when they should rise again to rid the country of the English. True the story is Arthurian, but such was the Welsh need for some hope, so utter was their desolation.

Perhaps Owain really was a magician who could become invisible and conjure the weather. Perhaps as a dragon he retired to a cave in Snowdonia for a long sleep to cure his weariness. Perhaps as an eagle he soared above the ridges of Pumlumon, searching for thermals to lift him high enough to view the field of Hyddgen.

WALES UNTIL 1536

In the aftermath of the war of Owain Glyndŵr, the English Parliament enacted laws which were framed to ensure that never again could the Welsh threaten an English king. If savage laws had not been sufficient to hold them down when revolt threatened, then clearly what were needed were laws that were even more savage and repressive. No man of Welsh parentage could buy land near a Marcher town, or be a citizen of such a town, or hold any office at all, or possess a weapon. No Welsh child could be apprenticed to trade or go to college. If there were lawsuits between an Englishman and a Welshman, then Englishmen must be judge and jury. If any Englishman were foolish enough to marry a Welshwoman, he would become Welsh in the eyes of the law. And finally, all gatherings of Welsh people were forbidden.

This last law was the most brutal because it denied the Welsh the opportunity to help each other at harvest. Their country had been ravaged, their sons killed. They were to be taxed to pay for the cost of the war – and now they could harvest no food. As if all that was not enough, Wales was home to many who had been raiders all their adult life and could not – or would not – stop. When what little you have is taken by your lord or by a bandit, there is little to do but weep or die.

Yet when Henry V, who had defeated the rebellion, called for men to fight for him in France, the old desire for a warrior king to love and admire was still strong, and Welsh bowmen won for him the battle of Agincourt. Henry V was a brilliant general: fearless and, best of all, victorious – a man every Celt could be proud to follow.

Not so Henry's son, Henry VI, who succeeded him when only nine months old. The long-term government of the state by a council of ministers left England full of ambitious lords, none more so than Richard Plantaganet, Duke of York, son of the sister of the Earl of March, whose uncle Edmund Mortimer had died for Glyndŵr in Harlech castle. In the power struggle that followed – the Wars of the Roses as it has become known – Wales saw action as an army raised by Owen and Jasper Tudur marched across country from Pembroke to defeat at Mortimer's Cross.

West Wales was staunchly Lancastrian and was invaded by land and sea for its beliefs: Jasper Tudur, having survived the battle, fled to Ireland. It is an irony that a descendant of the Mortimer family which sided with Glyndŵr should have been in a position to chastise a part of the country that so vigorously opposed his rebellion.

The Wars of the Roses had begun with the vacuum left by Henry V, that most powerful of kings, defeater of Glyndŵr and conqueror of France. After he died his young widow, Catherine of France, married a commoner – Owen Tudur of the Anglesey family which had captured Conwy castle and supported Glyndŵr. They had two children, Edmund and Jasper, the Earls of Richmond and Pembroke, legitimised by an Act of Parliament in 1453. Edmund Tudur married Margaret Beaufort, a descendant of John of Gaunt and heiress to the title of the family who had given England Henry IV. Their son Henry Tudur – Harri Tudur to the Welsh – was raised in France, since his existence represented a threat to Edward IV, the Yorkist king. When Edward died in 1483, his brother Richard III took the throne, entering history as the evil hunchback who murdered his nephews (and rightful heirs to the throne), the 'Princes in the Tower'.

On 7 August 1485 Henry Tudor landed in Pembrokeshire, and the Welsh rose to herald a new Welsh star rising to rescue them from oppression. The bards could recite the lineage of this Welshman, and point out the prophecies which foretold his coming and the victory that was bound to be his. Henry Tudor travelled north through Ceredigion (Cardiganshire) to Machynlleth, the Parliament town of Owain Glyndŵr. He then moved east through Powys to Welshpool and on to Shrewsbury and England. On 22 August he met Richard III at Bosworth. With Richard's defeat the Welsh gave England a king, Henry VII.

Fifty years later the second king of the house of Tudor, Henry VIII, united England and Wales. In the Act of Union Welshmen were given equal rights to Englishmen, since all became citizens of the new kingdom. English law was brought to Wales, replacing the laws of Hywel Dda, but replacing also the summary justice of the Marcher lords. In only one respect was the Union obviously against the interests of the Welsh – the English language was made the official, and only, language of the courts and administrators. This act put the Welsh language into a new, lesser light, which has broken many languages. But for some reason, and although it spent centuries in the wilderness, Cymraeg remained the true language of the people. Gradually, the noble born and sycophants found it more convenient to forget its existence for English was the vehicle that allowed ambitious Welsh people to 'get on'. But the vast majority continued to speak nothing but Welsh into the 20th century. It survived everything, including the use of the 'Welsh

76

Not' in schools. During the 19th century 'enlightened' educationalists hung a block of wood or slate engraved with the letters 'WN' around the neck of a child caught speaking his or her mother tongue. The Welsh Not was passed from child to child, encouraging tell-tales, because the one holding the block at the end of the week was harshly treated. A similar device, but a stick rather than a block, more or less killed the Gaelic tongue across vast swathes of Ireland during the same period. Welsh proved to be more resilient, maybe because the language became identified with being Welsh. Where the Irish had an island that they could call their own, Wales since 1282, apart from the time of Glyndŵr, had little more than its language and both it and the people refused to be broken on the English wheel. The language has fought a rearguard action in many places, but it was finally given joint status with English almost six centuries after Glyndŵr had sought to make it the language of government. Contrary to popular belief outside Wales, the language remains a National one, spoken across the country and at all levels of society. Owain Glyndŵr would have it no other way.

What Price Rebellion?

When Owain came to prominence in 1399 he was a relatively prosperous, cultured country gentleman. Undercurrents of sentiment against the English overlords were strong in the Wales in which he had lived until then, but open rebellion was not a likely event. When he disappeared, he was considered by authority to be a penniless rebel leaving a country that had been ravaged by hard years of brutal warfare. Did he therefore fail?

He took charge of a country that was at first divided but which was quickly fired by his successes. Most areas of the country came to support him and all of Wales was affected by his vision and by his military skills. The men who flocked to his side came from all sectors of society, and included English noblemen as well as English families that lived in Wales. Also, many Welsh former students from Oxford and Cambridge returned to fight for the freedom of their nation alongside farm workers and soldiers who had served with Owain, but then on behalf of the English king in Scotland and maybe France.

Owain utilised what many, in the main English chroniclers and historians, have since percieved as weaknesses, and turned them into great strengths. He fought the only campaign that offered any hope of success because he dared not fight the English army in open battle, for they had been trained and hardened in the killing fields of France. There they had humbled a nation with infinitely more resources than those of Wales, so what chance would his outnumbered and lightly clad warriors stand against such forces? Owain's genius was to train his men to strike quickly and escape from confrontation. He and his lieutenants knew and, more importantly, understood the terrain. They utilised the inclement weather to such an extent that English chroniclers deemed Owain supernatural. He saw also that it was better to have his men picking off stragglers and at the same time striking the fear of something even beyond God into the invading army as it lumbered about, huge and slow. But he also showed great military accumen when forced into pitched battles where his forces succeeded although vastly outnumbered. Examples of such were his use of the setting sun at Hyddgen and of the terrain at Bryn Glas.

His main tactics are now well known as guerrilla warfare, and Owain Glyndŵr's methods have undergone the scrutiny of other famous men who have successfully fought totally unbalanced fights against forces far bigger and more powerful than their own. Castro in Cuba and Grivas in Cyprus are two such guerrilla leaders who studied Glyndŵr's ways. Nearer to home, the RAF has also been known to cite his methods as exemplary in the process of training their cadets.

The English are said to have invented scorched earth policy in France to prevent their army from being followed across country by French troops. They were not slow to use the same policy in Wales, but were probably surprised to find the tactic used against themselves also. Wealth that might have helped equip Henry's invading force was removed, as was food that might feed it and anything that might shelter it. It was, of course, also of benefit to Owain's men that they should eat and that wealth was collected en route for war was, and continues to be, a very expensive pastime. The use of a scorched earth policy in Wales, by both sides, meant that almost all the major towns and monastic houses were looted and severe hardship was caused.

Such a policy however might not have been so strange in a time when moving an army of thousands meant living off the land, for storing supplies nearby and transporting it to marching troops was impractical. The loss of the few possessions that the people had could probably be made good in a short time, and people in times of war had long learned to hide something away, just in case, so as to survive until the next harvest. The Welsh had also lived for a century under English rule when taxes left them very little for themselves anyway.

English chroniclers and historians have made much of the

barbarity of Owain Glyndŵr, including his willingness to utilise the scorched earth policy, to kill Welshmen who opposed him, and to sanction the desecration of cropses. It is true that Owain attacked towns and killed people in Wales, but these were English towns where no Welsh man or woman had been allowed for over a century, although it is probable that Welsh supporters of the English system had started to infiltrate even these bastions of superiority by the end of the 14th century. There are no definite reports of the public desecration of corpses on Owain's part, but Hotspur and many others were drawn and quartered by the opposition, the remnants of the corpses to be dispersed as a warning to the corners of Henry IV's kingdom. There are contemporary records that Henry IV himself was present at Llanymddyfri when Llywelyn ap Gruffudd Fychan was 'put to death'. The reports of the desecration of English corpses, especially pertaining to their genitalia, by the female followers of Glyndŵr at Bryn Glas came into being a century and a half or more after the event. No contemporary reports mentioned these rumours, even though anti-Welsh propaganda was rife at the time.

War is dreadful, and in it the laws of society are suspended. But Glyndŵr's part in the war against England, and war it was although propaganda has always maintained that it was nothing more than a local rebellion, was certainly no worse than that of the other side. His soldiers behaved no differently to armies in other European conflicts of the period and indeed, a strong case can be made for saying that they were more civilised, if such a term can be justified to describe any army's behaviour in time of war.

Owain was not, by his own insistence, racist against the English although much has been made of his denouncement of 'Saxons' everywhere in his letters to his 'Celtic Cousins' in Scotland and Ireland. It is probably true however that he wished to ensure that all English leaders understood that Wales was no place for those likely to offer them support or shelter. He received incredible loyalty from all over the country, even following his use of scorched earth and all his supposed savagery, he was never once compromised. His head carried an enormous prize but no one Welshman anywhere turned traitor. Not once was he captured and, the legends of Hywel Sele and Dafydd Gam apart, not one of his own people attempted to kill him. The revolt did not come to an end when Glyndŵr left the limelight – but without him to the fore, it petered out. He was unfortunate in that he lacked a truly decisive victory in battle against the King himself, which would have shown his allies and compatriots that he was capable not only of keeping the English out, but for keeping them out for good.

This was not possible with his own troops, and attempts to do so with the French army were bound to fail. The Welsh did not like the French any more than they liked the English: they were merely a common enemy of the English at this particular time, as were their fellow Celts in Scotland and Ireland. The remnants of the French army that over-wintered in Wales soon convinced the Welsh that they were better off looking after their own affairs. The alliance with France was not based on a solid enough footing. Glyndŵr wanted France to conquer England and then go away, whilst France needed Wales as an overland route into England. Ultimately, if a French invasion had succeeded, Owain would have found, like Vortigern before him, that invited armies have a nasty tendency of not going home. The same can also be made of the Tri-partite Indenture. Intrigue and discord were more or less written into the text, and success was not a likely outcome for such an alliance had it come about following the Battle of Shrewsbury.

There are largely negative aspects of the war. At a time when warfare was often swift and brutal, most 'local rebellions' lasted little more than a few months. The war of Owain Glyndŵr lasted ten long years, during which the most revered of all Welsh leaders exposed a new vision of Wales. What was it about this strange, enigmatic man that persuaded the people to give virtually every last ounce of strength and drop of blood to the cause of ridding their country of an unwanted occupying force that had proved too strong on every previous occasion. This time they very nearly succeeded, but the English once again proved too resourceful.

What Glyndŵr promised was real, tangible freedom, and he set in motion a process that continues today. His parliament at Machynlleth took a step towards democracy that was truly revolutionary for its time. The parliaments of Owain Glyndŵr were the first on Welsh soil, and would not be repeated for nearly six hundred years. But Owain's vision did not end there. His desire for Welsh universities is of the greatest importance and shows that Owain recognised two things. The first was that, to be free of England in the fullest sense, Wales had to provide and maintain its own government, which in turn required the educating of Welshmen. He was concerned that the Welsh of Oxford should think well of him and gave money to many of those who joined him. But secondly he recognised that education was the way to free men's minds and that what his people needed was a change of attitude, a new way of thinking. Too long had they been slaves to the English. Owain would educate the young Welsh and send them home to teach not only their own children, but also their parents. His universities remained a dream in Wales for almost five centuries, but they were finally and reluctantly granted at the end of the 19th century. Another great vision was an independent church, but this also remained a dream until the early 1920s. Last, and probably most important of all, was his vision of Wales on a wider stage. He created contacts with other European countries that included, apart from France, Spain, Scotland and Ireland. All his other visions have come to fruition over the last century, some of them in the last two or three years. This vision of Wales in Europe is also coming true for the Welsh Assembly now has an office in Brussels.

One of the legends that grew about Owain Glyndŵr during

Tudor times was that, when walking from Glyndyfrdwy very early in the morning, he met the Abbot of Glyn-y-groes (Valle Crucis Abbey), also taking the early morning air. When Owain joked that the abbot had risen early, the abbot said no – it was Owain who had risen early … a century too early.

It is a lovely story and implies that he was the right man, but that he came at the wrong time. In retrospect we can see the failure to achieve a goal does not render the goal unworthy. Owain Glyndŵr's gift to the Welsh was the idea that the people are greater than the prince.

YNYS MÔN
(Anglesey)

Conwy

Caernarfon

Moel Hebog

Harlech

**Owain Glyndŵr's
Way**

Machynlleth

Aberystwyth

Hyddgen

Pumlumon

Llanidloes

Ceredigion

St David's

Carmarthen

Milford Haven

Laugharne

GOWER

Prestatyn

Offa's Dyke
National
Trail

Ruthin

Glyndyfrdwy

Sycharth

Shrewsbury

Y Trallwng/
Welshpool

Tref-y-Clawdd/
Knighton

Abbey
Cwmhir

Pilleth

Kentchurch

Grosmont

Usk

Chepsto

Cardiff

Owain Glyndŵr's Way

Knighton to Abbey Cwm-hir

The route that commemorates Owain Glyndŵr's name and explores the countryside of mid-Wales starts close to the site of his greatest military success, at Knighton, just a couple of miles north-east of Pilleth.

Knighton is a border market town, associated not only with our walk but also with the Offa's Dyke footpath, sitting as it does about half-way along that route and being the site of both the Offa's Dyke Heritage Centre (in West Street: the Centre doubles as the Tourist Information Office for the town) and the headquarters of the Offa's Dyke Association which promotes both the conservation of the dyke, the National Trail which follows it, and the country on either side of it.

But for all its market-town bustle and association with quiet days spent walking the local country, Knighton has a bloody past. Its position, on high ground controlling the narrowing of the Teme (Tafeidiad) valley, which was a gateway between Wales, and England, ensured that the town's site was strategically important from the time when the Saxons confronted the Cymry across what is now the border of Wales. Even before then this area may have been of military significance for Caer Caradog, 3 miles (5 kms) away to the north-east, is named for Caratacus, the British leader in the fight against invading Romans. As was once noted, 'The country around is eloquent of war and foray.'

It has been suggested that when Caer Caradog was occupied there was a smaller look-out fort at Bryn-y-Castell a little way east of the town centre. The early Norman lords at Knighton may have used the Bryn-y-Castell site, as indeed may Rhodri Mawr at an earlier date, but when it was raised, the stone-built

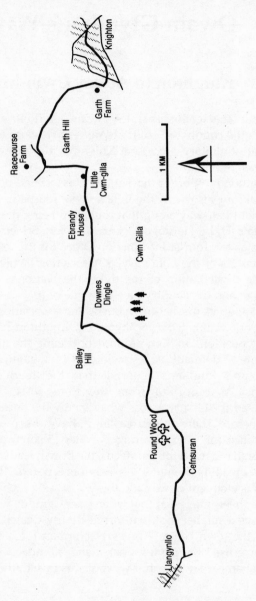

Knighton

Garth
Farm

Garth Hill

Racecourse
Farm

Little
Cwm-gilla

Ebrandy
House

Cwm Gilla

Downes
Dingle

Bailey
Hill

Round Wood

Cefnsuran

Llangynllo

1 KM

86

castle was on a site to the west of the town's centre. This castle was raised by the Mortimers, but seems to have been small, perhaps because of the closeness of another castle at nearby Knucklas. Both were constructed at the turn of the twelfth century, but neither survived the 1262 campaign of Llywelyn ap Gruffudd. When relative peace returned the Mortimers restored Knighton Castle, but it was destroyed again – and this time for good – when Glyndŵr came this way in 1402: Owain came from the west and 'there is scarce a house left standing between Llanidloes and Knighton'.

The Mortimers were a powerful Marcher family, with ambitions to be king-makers and, occasionally, kings. Roger Mortimer was exiled to France by Edward II and there lived with Isabella, Edward's queen, and her son, the future Edward III. He formed an army which invaded England in 1326 and won power, capturing Edward. It was probably on Mortimer's instructions that the king was murdered at Berkeley Castle in Gloucestershire and for a time the Marcher lord was the power in England. Ultimately Edward III recognised the threat posed by Roger's arrogance and he was arrested and executed at London's Tyburn, near what is now Marble Arch.

But the family did not learn any lessons from this and in 1461 it was another Mortimer, Edward, who commanded the Yorkist army at Mortimer's Cross, 16 kilometres (10 miles) south-east, where the Lancastrian army was utterly defeated. A Welsh captain of the defeated army was beheaded and his head placed on the steps of Hereford Cathedral, where 'a mad woman combed his hair and washed away the blood from his face, and got candles and set them round his head, all burning, more than a hundred'. Was she mad or clairvoyant? The man's grandson was to turn the tables on his grandfather's executioners and to found a dynasty. For the mad woman tended the head of Owen Tudur.

The new peace allowed the Marcher lands to be brought under the control of England's government, and while this

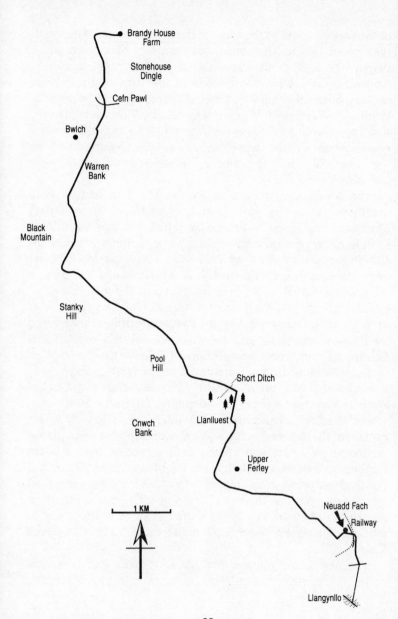

Brandy House
Farm

Stonehouse
Dingle

Cefn Pawl

Bwlch

Warren
Bank

Black
Mountain

Stanky
Hill

Pool
Hill

Short Ditch

Cnwch
Bank

Llanlluest

Upper
Ferley

1 KM

Neuadd Fach

Railway

Llangynllo

88

seemed to finally end Welsh hopes for independence it did bring stability into the lives of the ordinary folk whose misfortune it had been to be born into the area. Knighton was at first placed in the country of Shropshire, but transferred to Radnorshire by the Act of Union of 1536: its Norman market charter and position right on the new Welsh-English border ensured that it became prosperous. In 1854 the market witnessed Radnorshire's last case of wife-selling when a local man led in his wife with a rope around her neck. Another man bid a shilling, the seller being so pleased with the bargain that he threw in the rope as well.

Today Knighton is a picturesque old market town set on the side of a hill, around a clock tower very reminiscent of the one in Machynlleth which constitutes the half-way mark on our route. The Welsh inhabitants of Knighton today, shopping in the steeply sloping Tudor 'Narrows' - the town's most picturesque street - may not be aware that their distant ancestors would have walked in fear at the same spot. Once a Welshman caught east of Offa's Dyke had an ear cut off, and the dyke put Knighton knoll in England. Its line is followed by Offa's Road from the B4355 to the Castle site. From the B4355 to the river the Dyke runs along Conjuror's Drive, a link with the time not so long ago when this area of Radnorshire was famous for its wizards or conjurors, skilled in the curing of animals and people by spell-casting.

Glyndŵr's Way starts at the clock tower, the first steps being uphill along what remains of High Street and The Narrows. At the top turn right and descend to reach a path beside the Wilcome (Wylcwm) Brook. Turn right along this path, but soon bear right again, leaving the stream to climb between houses. Cross the main road (Penybont Road) and continue along the path opposite (Middle Garth Path) which makes its way around the northern flank of Garth Hill. At first there are good views back towards Knighton, but then the path disappears into fine woodland. Turn left when the path reaches a minor road. Soon,

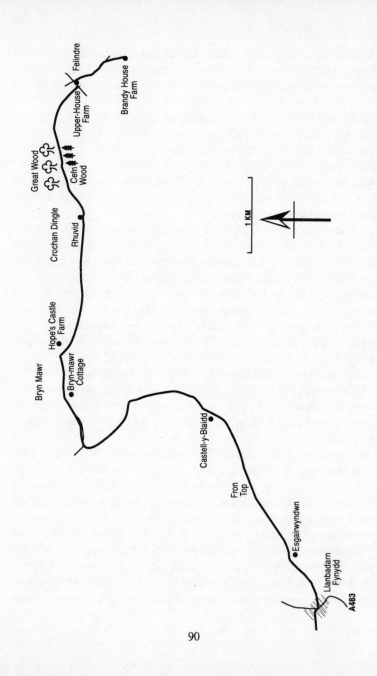

Felindre

Brandy House
Farm

Upper-House
Farm

Great Wood

Cefn
Wood

Crochan Dingle

Rhuvid

Hope's Castle
Farm

Bryn Mawr

Bryn-mawr
Cottage

Castell-y-Blaidd

Fron
Top

Esgairwyndwn

Llanbadarn
Fynydd

A483

1 KM

90

to the right, Racecourse Farm is a reminder that until 1861 there was a race-course on the high flat summit of the hill beyond it, to the west. Below the hill is Knucklas (Cnwclas) where there was also a Norman castle. Before the Norman castle there was another, lived in by the son of Uther Pendragon of Crugybyddar at Felindre, to the north-west and on our route. Uther's son, Arthur, went to the assistance of two brothers, freeing them from their imprisonment by giants. The boys' father, Gogfran Gawr, himself a giant from Brecon, was so thrilled that he offered Arthur his daughter, Gwynhwyfar, in marriage. Arthur and Guinevere (the English form of her name) lived in his castle at Knucklas, and it was from there that Arthur set out to free Britain from the Saxons and to found his Round Table of Knights. When in the nineteenth century a great slab was lifted at a mound near Monaughty Poeth, just the other side of the Teme from Knucklas, the excavators found the skeletons of five tall men.

Vavasour Powell, the governor of churches in the border region under the Long Parliament which followed the Civil War was born at Knucklas. He was a man of strong, sometimes contradictory, opinions who quarrelled with most people in authority at some time. He supported Cromwell, was later imprisoned by him and finally died in Fleet prison after the Restoration.

Follow the road downhill, bearing left once, turning right at the bottom to follow Ebrandy Lane past Little Cwm-Gilla. Continue along the lane when the metalling ends, climbing steadily up Bailey Hill. There are fine views southwards now, especially where the track traverses the upper end of Downe's Dingle. Beyond this, continue for another 250m to a track junction. Turn left (south) here, following the field edge track, uphill at first, then descending steadily. To the north are some old quarries close to which lies the Siwan Ellis (Phil Price) Rally School where potential future world champions learn their craft. In spring the foxgloves and rosebay willowherb are superb in this area.

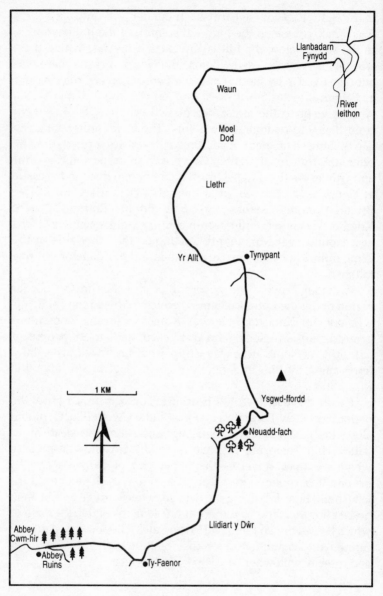

Llanbadarn
Fynydd

Waun

River
Ieithon

Moel
Dod

Llethr

Yr Allt   ●Tynypant

▲

Ysgwd-ffordd

●Neuadd-fach

1 KM

Llidiart y Dŵr

Abbey
Cwm-hir

●Abbey
Ruins

●Ty-Faenor

From Cefnsuran, the Way follows field paths to reach a road close to Llangynllo. Turn right to follow the road into this attractive little village. The village is named for the fifth or sixth century Celtic St Cynllo to whom the church is also dedicated. It is likely that Cynllo had a hermit cell here, though nothing of that now exists. That can be said with certainty, though the date of the present church is much less certain. There are features from the 13th century - a lancet window in the north wall - and the 15th century, but much of the rest is later, dating from a major rebuild in the 19th century. The sturdy, but excellent, tower was built in 1894.

To the north of the village, on top of Fron-goch, a hill spur pointing towards the River Lugg a curious ceremony was enacted periodically until the early years of the twentieth century. The collector of a pair of ancient taxes was elected by auction, the lowest offer for the wage required for the job being accepted. There is nothing particularly unusual about that, you may say, since the idea of accepting the lowest tender for collecting taxes or tolls is well-known. But here the auction was held in a slit trench, the final deal being made when all parties concerned joined hands in a hole dug at the end of the trench. Photographs exist of the ceremony – groups of well-dressed, earnest men clasping hands while standing waist-deep in a hole, surrounded by equally well-dressed and earnest spectators. They look like stills from a surreal comedy sketch.

Turn right along the minor road just beyond the church, following it to a junction with another minor road. Go straight across, but soon turn left along a bridleway. Where this reaches a road, go ahead, soon crossing the Heart of Wales railway. Just beyond, turn left (towards Neuadd Fach), following a bridleway across fields to reach a green lane. The lane is superb, beautifully sited on a level ridge with lovely views in all directions. To the north is the scattered hamlet of Ferley (named from the Welsh *fferllyd*, meaning 'cold' in the sense of exposed to the elements, which is an appropriate description). The bridleway descends to reach a crossing track. Here the Way heads north along a track that eventually bears left (west) to reach the ancient, heather-covered rampart of Short Ditch. The name is apt, the structure being only a few hundred metres long. It is said to be the remains of a defence thrown up in 1402 by Edmund Mortimer to protect Knighton from Owain Glyndŵr. If that is true, then it is astonishing - the ditch is 10 kilometres (6 miles) from Knighton; if a circular defence was planned it would have been more than 60 kilometres (40 miles) around, and it would have needed to be continuous or else Glyndŵr would simply have gone round behind it. The manpower required to complete and man such a defence would have been colossal. Perhaps Mortimer anticipated a mountain-route advance, or, as many experts believe, it formed part of an ancient Saxon system that predated Offa's Dyke.

Beyond Short Ditch, the Way breaks out on to open hill, the heather-topped flanks of Pool and Stanky Hills, and Black Mountain. This is marvellous walking country with great views in good weather. In poor weather it is altogether a more trying place, though there is the possibility of escape to the salvation of an exposed lane to the west. At the col between Stanky Hill and Black Mountain – though the lowest of the three peaks we have passed it is the one mountain among hills – the Way leaves the bridleway and heads north, avoiding the summit by a route along the eastern flank to reach another bridleway on Warren Bank, which it follows to a minor road at Cefn Pawl. The road heads east to Bugeildy, birthplace of Ieuan Ddu or Black Jack, a famous local conjuror. As Dr John Dee he became Elizabeth I's tutor, a man respected at court as an eminent mathematician – as well as astrologer – of his day. It is likely that Shakespeare used this Radnor wizard as the model for Prospero.

The Way does not go to Bugeildy, heading north along the bridleway to reach the edge of Mill Wood. The bridleway follows the wood edge and then heads east to Brandy House Farm. Go down the farm lane to a road and turn left into

Felindre where there is an inn, but little else. At the cross-roads beyond the inn, turn left, but soon right to reach Upper House Farm from where a bridleway climbs a ridge spur to the woodland above Crugybyddar and the Teme valley. Two mounds here, on opposite banks of the River Teme (Afon Tafeidiad), are the legendary home of Uther Pendragon, Arthur's father. 'Pendragon' means 'dragon's head,' dragon being used to distinguish this warlord from others who had different wild-beast names. Some have suggested that here is the origin of the Welsh dragon symbol.

Beyond the wood above the Teme is Rhuvid from where a bridleway leads westward, gently climbing the Rhuvid Bank to Hope's Castle Farm and continuing west from there along the farm road. Where the road turns sharp right, turn left along a byway, following it south to reach the hummocks that are all that remain of Castell-y-Blaidd. The castle is a 'ringwork', a poorly understood construction which is believed to be Norman, but may be earlier. In form it is an earthwork horseshoe, but was the hole in the ring left deliberately, because the site was unfinished, because of destruction by enemy action or simply as a result of later farming? The mystery is deepened by the existence of a platform site to the south-west which shows the remains of four houses. Could these have been Norman or are they, too, earlier?

From the castle, which is well-sited to guard a crossing of ancient tracks (one of which heads north to the ancient site of Rhiw Porthnant where there are two Bronze Age round barrows and another, more curious, barrow with a flat top, a mound known locally as Dicky's Stool), the Way turns south-west, following a bridleway to reach a minor road: follow this, or the path beside it, to Llanbadarn Fynydd.

Research earlier this century suggested that two stories from the *Mabinogion* could be fairly accurately placed in this area of Radnorshire (Maesyfed), and an extension of this research suggested that some of the campaigns fought by Arthur against the Saxons could also be associated with the same place. It has even been suggested that Llanbadarn could be the site of Mons Badonicus, Mount Badon, where Arthur fought the twelfth battle – the last and greatest – of his campaign against the Saxons. There is no evidence anywhere in Britain for the true battle site, though there are projected sites from Scotland to Dorset, the currently favoured one being on the Ridgeway path in Wiltshire. On the basis of the name alone, Badon, there are countless potential sites, but Llanbadarn is not one of these since its name is well understood as being from *llan*, the normal 'church' prefix of many Welsh names, and Padarn, the sixth-century disciple of David. The second word addition to the name is a mutation of *mynydd*, for Padarn's church here was set among the hills.

But if Arthur had fought at Badon he would surely have had as his castle – if not his battlefield – the conical hill three kilometres (2 miles) south of Llanbadarn on which sits Castell Dinboeth. It is also known as Maud's Castle, named for Roger Mortimer's widow after he had built it in the thirteenth century. Though the site bears a thirteenth-century Norman name, it had a long Welsh pedigree before that and there is evidence of a very ancient hill-fort. The hillside is impressively steep, the inhabitants of the castle on its flat top paying for their security with a stiff approach climb. On the summit the remains are at once poor yet impressive. There is a rock-cut ditch, littered with the stones of long-gone walls, and a single chunk of thick wall, shaped like a sea stack, high above it. The final destruction is thought to have been by Llywelyn ap Gruffudd. The views from the site are impressive.

Since we have ventured from our route, let us go a little way further, still southward. At Llananno church there is arguably the finest rood screen in Wales. It dates from the turn of the sixteenth century and is a beautifully executed and inventive background with niches containing figures of Christ, the apostles and prophets. The figures are late nineteenth-century replacements, the prophets wearing sashes with their names, like modern beauty queens.

South again at Llanbister is another fine church. The beauty here lies in the way that successive architects have used the hilly site to add interest to the building, for it is a maze of levels and steps. There are steps up in the porch, and again inside to the level of the nave, then more steps to the ancient gallery and steps down to an unusual feature: a baptistery for total immersion.

Both churches are well-sited: Llananno is beside Afon Ieithon, and Llanbister on its hill. Llanbadarn church is also well set beside Afon Ieithon and the Way passes it as it heads west. Follow the main road south, then turn right on a lane past the church. St Padarn's has a delightful bellcote and some surviving 15th century work, though much of what exists dates from a major restoration in 1894. Inside the head beam of the rood screen still exists, showing carvings that are reminiscent of those at Llananno.

The lane to the church crosses Afon Ieithon and continues around a long, tight left-hand bend to a cross-roads. Here turn right (westward) up a stony track, following it to where it ends on the flank of Garn Hill. Now go around the head of the shallow valley to the south to the col between Castle Bank and Moel Dod. Here the route turns south, skirting (or climbing) Moel Dod and crossing fine open common to reach Ty'n-y-pant. During the last stages of this section of the Way, Castell Dinboeth dominates the view eastward.

Take the farm lane to a minor road, cross and follow a bridleway as it climbs across another section of common land below the triangulated summit above Ysgwd-ffordd. The short detour to the summit is worthwhile for the fine views west and east.

From the col south of the peak the Way heads west, steeply down to and through the Neuadd-fach woods, over the Bachell brook and on to a road. Turn left along the road for about 2.5

kilometres (1.5 miles) to reach a signed path on the right. Just beyond this turn a short detour leads to Ty-Faenor, a manor house built with stone from Abbey Cwm-hir.

The path takes the Wayfarer across fields and a stream, and along a short section of forest track to emerge on to a road. Follow this into Abbey Cwm-hir.

Abbey Cwm-hir to Llanidloes

Abbey Cwm-hir was built for Cistercian monks, an order founded at Citeaux in France by St Robert of Molesmes on the feast of St Benedict in 1098. Each abbot of a Cistercian house made an annual pilgrimage to Citeaux and this, with the Cistercians' love for solitude, has led to some quite superb buildings, all of them beautifully sited. Think of Fountains and Rievaulx and of this spot in the quiet Clywedog valley.

Cwm-hir was founded in 1143, but this was a short-lived venture and it was re-founded by one Cadwallon ap Madog, a cousin of Rhys ap Gruffudd, Prince of South Wales, in 1176. Some stories tell of a joint founding with Roger Mortimer and William Fitzalan, two Norman Marcher lords. This would seem strange, as the March lands were subject to the almost continuous bickering between the Welsh and their new neighbours at that time. The Norman lords were, however, a very pious breed and the simple dignity of the sheep-farming Cistercians would certainly have appealed to the Welsh. Perhaps the site's remoteness and its spirituality allowed it to become a symbol of peace to both sides. The son and grandson of Cadwallon also endowed the abbey, whose monks had come from the mother church of Hendy-gwyn (Whitland). Some idea of the strange times in which the abbey grew up, and of the strange bedfellows the co-founders made – if indeed they were co-founders – is evidenced by the fact that Cadwallon's son Hywel, after endowing the abbey with extra land, was executed at Bridgnorth in 1212 for the murder of a Norman lord. Later in 1231 the abbey may have become involved in the feud between Llywelyn Fawr and Henry III. I say 'may,' because the true casualty of Henry's action has not been reliably identified. Henry was at Hereford with his army, preparing to pursue Llywelyn who was near Montgomery Castle. It is said that Llywelyn persuaded an abbot to tell some of Henry's men that he knew of the prince's position. These men, convinced that

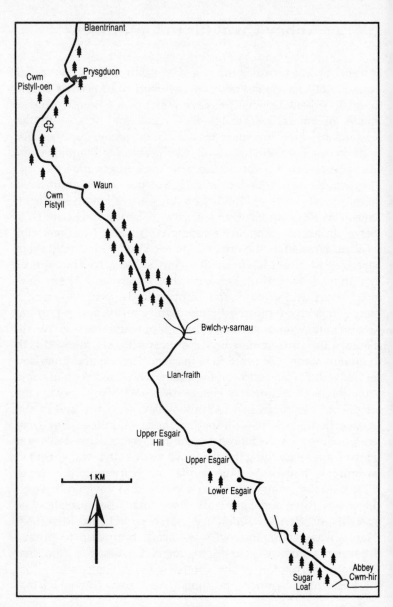

Blaentrinant

Cwm
Pistyll-oen   Prysgduon

Cwm
Pistyll   Waun

Bwlch-y-sarnau

Llan-fraith

Upper Esgair
Hill

Upper Esgair

Lower Esgair

1 KM

Sugar   Abbey
Loaf   Cwm-hir

they had caught Llywelyn off-guard, hurried on horseback to the site but became trapped in the treacherous quagmire of a water meadow and were slaughtered. The outraged Henry plundered and burnt the abbot's grange and fired the abbey. But which abbey? The story talks of Cumira, but is that Cwm-hir, or Cymer near Dolgellau? Cwm-hir is 40 kilometres (25 miles) from Montgomery (Trefaldwyn) and about 65 kilometres (40 miles) from Hereford, while Cymer is 55 kilometres (35 miles) and 160 kilometres (100 miles) distant respectively. On distance along it seems that if the story has any truth at all, it is more likely to be centred around Cwm-hir. Certainly there is architectural evidence that one period of building ceased around 1230. Some restoration probably took place, as it did again after the destruction of the Glyndŵr period.

Leland, the early sixteenth-century travel writer, said of Cwm-hir that 'no church in Wales is seen of such length as the foundations of the walls there begun doth show, but the third part of the work was never finished'. Of the projected work only the nave was completed, and that was 74 metres (242 feet) long, an enormous length approached by no other Cistercian abbey and by very few minsters and cathedrals. The existing marked out base area is 78 metres (255 feet) by 22 metres (73 feet). The nave was constructed with fourteen arched bays, four more than exist at Wells Cathedral and, according to expert judgement, equalling Canterbury in their splendour as a colonnade in early English design. The abbey was built for sixty monks and, despite its endowments, it was never a wealthy abbey, maintaining the austerity sought by its Order's founding monks but forgotten by many of the English abbeys. When Henry VIII's Dissolution came, in 1536, there were only three monks and the abbey and its lands were valued at £24 19s 4d. The abbey building passed at one remove to the Fowlers, a rich local family, a later member of which built Ty-Faenor with abbey stone. It was usual for the first owner after Dissolution to strip out any roof lead, a process which started a decay that was hastened by the use of the site as a local quarry for good-quality dressed stone. At Cwm-hir we can be grateful for one profound departure from this norm for, although the abbey itself was plundered (even the Hall opposite the site is of abbey stones, and it was not built until the 1830s) five of the nave bays were used in the reconstruction of Llanidloes church in 1542. The stones were not properly labelled and are not therefore in perfect original form, and one bay had to be narrowed - presumably because somebody got the measurements wrong - but the glory is still there to see. Imagine what a double row of fourteen bays would have looked like - three times the length of the Llanidloes nave.

The abbey ruins lie on private land, though access to them is allowed. There is a memorial tree above the site to a local angler, one of many who fish what was once the monks' pool. There is also a memorial - in the form of a slate gravestone - to Llywelyn ap Gruffudd. In 1282 Llywelyn died in a skirmish near Builth and the English king he had defied barbarously cut off the Welsh prince's head to exhibit it in a freak show in London. But what of the body? The monastic chronicles of Worcester and Chester – widely separate places – and much oral tradition has it that the body was brought here to Cwm-hir and that in the church the last true-born Prince of Wales (Glyndŵr could trace a lineage to the Royal houses, but was not true-born) was buried. No gravestone has ever been found for Llywelyn no headless body has ever been unearthed, but it seems likely that he is here: the memorial grave slab reflects that belief.

Cwm-hir is a quiet, peaceful spot. No one could object to the cows which browse among the ruined walls, but there is something disturbing about the caravans and the scrap metal heap which share the site.

Today the visitor to Abbey Cwm-hir who knows nothing of the ruins sees the beauty and experiences the peace of the Clywedog valley, and notices the inn sign and the new church. He misses the Abbey of the Blessed Virgin Mary altogether. The inn is the 'Happy Union', the sign being a man with a leek in his hat riding on a goat.

The church (opposite the inn), is of an unusual design from the middle of the last century: the spire is curious, octagonal with wooden slats almost like a dovecote.

From the village the National Trail follows a short section of the Monk's Way, an ancient pathway that linked Cwm-hir to the Abbey of Strata Florida (Ystrad Fflur), near Pontrhydfendigaid. That walk, crossing the beautiful wilderness of Elenydd between the Elan and Claerwen reservoirs, is worthwhile but its exploration is another story.

The Monk's Way follows a bridleway through pleasant woodland to reach a footbridge over the Clywedog brook and a minor road. Across the road, field paths take the Wayfarer past the farms of Cwmysgawen and Lower and Upper Esgair, climbing steadily up Upper Esgair Hill with an expanding view to the north. At the top of the climb, beyond the shallow summit of Llan-fraith, to the right, the path joins a track. To the left this track leads up to Castell-y-garn, a burial chamber set on the highest point of the local hills. When excavated the chamber, which dates from the Bronze Age, was found to contain a chest of human bones. Glyndŵr's Way does not visit the chamber, turning right along the track to descend into Bwlch-y-sarnau, a small windswept hamlet named for its col-like position where paths met as they crossed the wild moorland.

Beyond the hamlet there is a really fine piece of country, not pretty in the sense of Cwm-hir, nor wild in the sense of high moor, but a combination of the two. There are trees, but these are pinched by the wind, and the fields have a bleak look about them. It is a strangely beautiful, twilight land, and with it comes the first view of high Wales, the ranges of Pumlumon and Cadair Idris beyond Afon Hafren the Severn's source.

The route leaves Bwlch-y-sarnau along a track known locally as the Roman Road, then heads north-west through a forestry plantation to reach a minor road at a T-junction. Continue north-

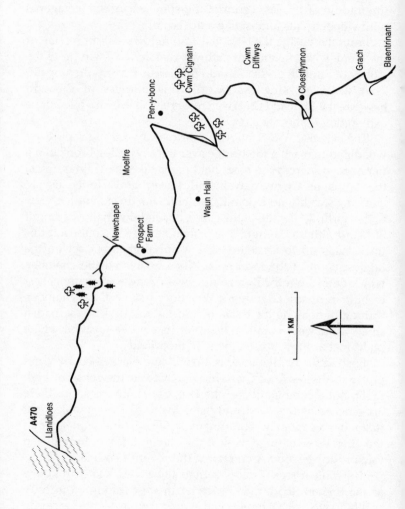

A470
Llanidloes

Newchapel

Prospect
Farm

Moelfre

Pen-y-bonc

Waun Hall

Cwm Cignant

Cwm
Diffwys

Cloesffynnon

Grach

Blaentrinant

1 KM

west along the road ahead, to reach a continuation of the plantation, beyond which the route is signed right (north-east) along a bridleway at the plantation's far edge. Follow the track to Prysgduon and on to Blaentrinant where the Rhydyclwydau brook formed the border between the old counties of Maesyfed and Trefaldwyn (Radnor and Montgomery). On the final section the view north-east ópens up as the Way contours around the scarp-like edge of Rhyddhywel plateau.

Beyond Blaentrinant the route takes a devious meandering way, following a minor road at first, then passing Grach farm and heading north-west, then west to reach another minor road. Turn right, passing Cloesffynnon and then following a track north towards Cwm farm. The farm is not reached however, the Way turning sharply left to follow and cross a stream. It now zig-zags north and west, passing the isolated cottage of Moelfre. This is a very pleasant section of the route, with striking views of the Dethenydd mountains, especially in the first stages, and excellent close views of wooded valleys as the Way passes Blaen-y-cwm to reach a minor road at Ashfield. Turn right, soon reaching Prospect Farm - the prospect from the farm is of Cwm Hafren (the Severn valley) and is well worth the name - and bearing right to Newchapel.

The new chapel was built in 1740 by an amalgamation of Non-conformist faiths, but rapidly became Baptist only. Behind us is Old Chapel Hill, whose name is not only interesting because of our position here at Newchapel, but also because it was where – according to the local stationmaster when talking to the Reverend Francis Kilvert – Edward I signed a peace treaty with the Welsh. There is no proof that this was the case, but it is an interesting example of the snippets which Kilvert collected into his famous diaries. Kilvert is rightly associated with the Wye Valley, Clyro and Bredwardine, but he also served at the church in St Harmon a few kilometres south of us, so there are sections of this diary which deal with the local area.

From Newchapel, the Way follows the minor road north-west, then uses a path to cross the Nant y Bradnant valley, a glorious section of country, before following another minor road into Llanidloes. On this final section into the town the road lies close to the Llety Cochnant stream which is on its way to the Severn. The stream is the red brook, its waters stained by haematite.

Llanidloes to Machynlleth

At the time of Arthur – that is, in the first half of the sixth century – the land here at the last ford of Afon Hafren (the Severn) was controlled by Llawfrodedd Goch, one of the three herdsmen of the cattle of Mudd Hael, a Celtic god. His grandson Idloes was a famously pious holy man in the early part of the seventh century and, with that eye for a nice spot which so characterises the early Celtic saints, he had his *llan* here, on the southern bank of the Severn and at the geographical centre of Wales.

There was an early market at the town which grew up around the *llan* – a market was the panacea for an ailing township, its most envied possession – and the centre of Llanidloes is still the Market Hall. But before that there was, of course, the Norman castle, perpetuated now only in the name of the Mount Inn on the road to Llangurig and the Wye Valley (Dyffryn Gwy). It is to the Market Hall, however, that the tourist – newcomer and aficionado alike – returns. It is an elegant structure, timber framed with one end of stone and the other of brick, and a bell turret complete with bell and weather-vane. The bell once rang at eight in the evening to tell the tradesmen to close their shops. It has had no clapper for many years now, though it was rung with a poker in 1900 to announce the relief of Mafeking.

The building dates from the late sixteenth century and is now the oldest timber-framed market hall in Wales, withstanding not only the test of time but also its precarious siting in the middle of what was, until the building of the bypass, a busy trunk road. Despite its name it has been many things: one end, the crib, was the town jail; it was a courthouse, a meeting house for Quakers, Wesleyans – John Wesley himself preached outside it, from a stone which can still be seen – and Baptists; it was also library and working men's institute; and a meeting place for local Chartists before their riot in the town.

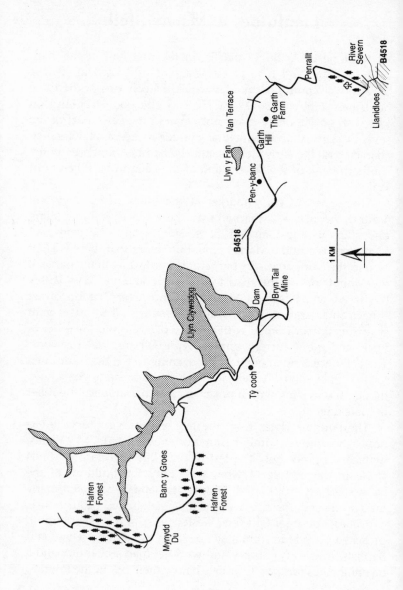

108

The Chartists supported the People's Charter, a six-point plan for electoral reform. Today the points at issue, such as payment of MPs, total franchise etc. appear commonplace. Five points have been granted and the sixth – annual parliaments – is not taken seriously by any credible party. But in 1839, the idea of the Charter appalled those who controlled the government, smelling of social justice, the abolition of privilege and other such malodorous reforms. The Chartists were clearly dangerous revolutionaries, to be treated accordingly. In general the civil strife that accompanied Chartism was most pronounced in working-class areas such as south Wales, where an uprising at Newport led to deaths and transportation, and here at the heart of the Welsh woollen industry. In 1833 there were eighteen fulling mills at the town.

In Llanidloes the Chartists were bitterly opposed by the town mayor, Thomas Marsh, because they threatened to disturb his monopoly on local power. He inflamed an already hot situation by importing three London constables and appointing three hundred local special constables when he heard the inhabitants had guns and were drilling on the hills. He paraded his men on 29 April 1839 and the next day a meeting of angry Chartists took place at the Market Hall. The mob had a few weapons and Marsh, either in a calculated move to provoke a riot he could crush or in order to escape a crowd that frightened him, broke a window and shouted 'The people for ever!' If riot he sought, riot he got. One London bobby was beaten and badly hurt, the other two escaping, and the mob controlled Llanidloes until 4 May.

The occupation was peaceable – one man was ducked in the Severn for suspected stealing – but could not last. Troops arrived from Brecon to be met, as it was later said, by 'a rusty pistol… soapsuds… and women's tongues'. Thirty-two men were arrested, some of whom were sentenced to a savage fifteen years' transportation.

Though the Market Hall is the most photographed town

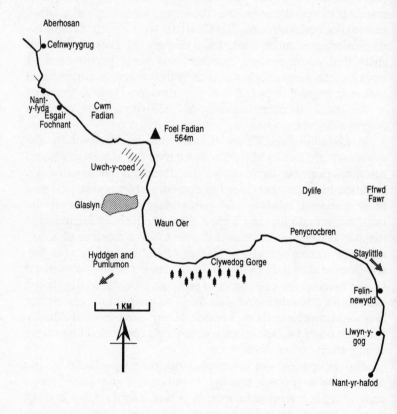

Aberhosan

Cefnwyrygrug

Nant-y-fyda

Esgair Fochnant

Cwm Fadian

Foel Fadian 564m

Uwch-y-coed

Glaslyn

Waun Oer

Dylife

Ffrwd Fawr

Penycrocbren

Staylittle

Hyddgen and Pumlumon

Clywedog Gorge

Felin-newydd

Llwyn-y-gog

1 KM

Nant-yr-hafod

110

building, there are others that should not be missed. Nearby is a superb half-timbered building (Elizabethan? No, 1926!) and Perllandy, meaning orchard house, on the Llangurig road is an almost unique example of a mid-seventeenth-century merchant's dwelling. The church of St Idloes has already been mentioned, built as it is with bays from Abbey Cwm-hir. Many consider it to be the finest church in Powys and it is certainly an interesting building with its modern extension tacked on to the ancient framework. If you walk twelve times around it on a special night, it is said you may look through the keyhole of the door to read the list of next year's dead. But which night is it that is so special?

There is also a Roman Catholic church, with a dedication to St Richard Gwyn, a local schoolmaster in the reign of Elizabeth I. He refused to take the oath of supremacy and to attend church and spent four years in jail; he was tortured and finally fined heavily. When asked how he would pay, he smiled and said, 'I have somewhat towards it – sixpence.' The joke went badly and he was sentenced to the full medieval execution, to be 'drawn on a hurdle to the place of execution where he shall hang half dead, and so be cut down alive, his members cast into the fire, his belly ripped unto the breast, his head cut off, his bowels, liver, lungs, heart thrown likewise into the fire...' and so on. Gwyn asked, 'What is all this? Is it any more than one death?' It was not. In 1970 Gwyn was canonised, the only local Catholic saint. How would he have felt about the man who, half a century before his bloody end in 1584, sold 'pardons all hot from Rome' in the town market?

Beside its architecture and its place in the social history of Wales, Llanidloes is also rich in fairy-lore. Near Llyn Ebyr, five kilometres (3 miles) north-west of the town, a shepherd and his wife had twin sons exchanged for fairy children. The wife, alarmed by the sudden change of her children to ugly, grumpy babies, consulted the Llanidloes wise man. He suspected changelings and told her to prepare soup in eggshells for the local farm workers, and then to listen carefully. When the babies saw this they spoke quietly to each other about the oddness of eggshells as soup bowls, thus giving themselves away, and were promptly thrown into the lake. The fairies rushed to their rescue and restored the original twins to their parents.

The town was famous for its conjurors, its *dynion hysbys* or cunning men. One once flew home to Cardiganshire from the town, taking with him a twelve-year-old boy who only realised why the journey had been so quick when he saw his garter at the top of a nearby ash tree. The conjurors offered cures for all complaints: to cure bed-wetting in children, give them gravy made from roast mouse; shingles could be cured by blood from a tom-cat's ear and warts by rubbing with the slime of a snail that was then impaled on a thorn. As the snail shrivelled, so would the wart! Finally, before leaving the town it might be worth finding a ladybird as a local saying is associated with releasing the insect – 'Ladybird, tell me what the weather will be. If foul then fall to the ground: if fair, then fly in the air.'

Glyndŵr's Way leaves Llanidloes along Long Bridge Street. There are two bridges in the town: Short Bridge at the end of Short Bridge Street crosses Afon Hafren before Clywedog has joined it. The Long Bridge is beyond the confluence, an elegant structure and much less dangerous to the visitor. Lady Jeffreys, a local gentlewoman who died in the eighteenth century, became a water spirit and was 'prayed down' into a bottle and put in the river under Short Bridge. In 1848, when the new bridge was built, a boy found the bottle with its fly-like inhabitant buzzing angrily. Luckily his parents made him put the bottle back, and it is still there to tempt the unwary.

The Way follows the B4518 signposted for Clywedog and Machynlleth, but soon turns right along a footpath which goes through Allt Goch Wood and around a golf course to reach a minor road. Go straight over and follow a path to another road, beyond which is The Garth farm. The Way does not reach the farm, bearing right to climb past Pen-y-banc to reach the B4518 again. Turn right and follow the road for a short distance, with a superb view across the old workings of the lead mine and the old village of terraced cottages of Y Fan. Lead was found here by chance in 1862 and it quickly became apparent that it was one of the richest lodes in Wales – and at a relatively accessible point, being only a few kilometres from the Severn valley. By the early 1870s the mine was producing quality ore in quantity, a £5 initial capital share being valued at £100. Sadly the prosperity was not to last for by 1878 the world price of lead had fallen and by 1880 the richest lodes were all but worked out. Thereafter the story of Y Fan was the sorry tale of all the Welsh metal mines – an unhappy list of new companies, bankruptcies and reduced output. In 1921 the mine closed for good. The site is now a delight for the industrial archaeologist. There is an old railway (dating from 1871) to trace as it goes east to join the main line at Caersws, the row of terraced cottages and the site spoil itself. The lake, Llyn y Fan, is said to have been formed by waste-heaps rather than being natural and is likely to have served as a small reservoir for the site.

The Way turns left off the road, following a path to the Bryn Tail mine site, another old lead mine. The ruins are open at any reasonable time, an information board outlining the mining process and identifying the various parts of the site. The mine was worked from at least the early eighteenth century (when its English owners, ignoring the Welsh pronunciation, called it Printile). At that time it was noted that the 'diced lead-ore' is 'very ponderous and rich; found about 3 Fathoms deep in Clay.' By the 1770s the mine had been long disused, but was restarted spasmodically, both for the mining of lead and also for barytes (barium sulphate) which was used in the manufacture of paint. The mine also yielded witherite (barium carbonate), a rare mineral, though this was never exploited commercially. As an aside, where Glyndŵr's Way turns left off the B4518, to the right is Pen y clun which was also once a mine site (after, it is said, the farmer's son announced that lead had been found there when he was drunk one night: his father, the farm owner, had wanted to keep the discovery secret, a strange decision as selling the land for mining was likely to be more profitable than working it). Pen y clun mine had one of the richest deposits of witherite ever found in Wales.

The Bryn Tail site and the Way are overlooked by the huge Clywedog dam. The dam is an impressive structure, irrespective of the merits or demerits of its position and the existence of the reservoir it holds back. The facts associated with such structures are awesome. It is 72 metres (237 feet) high and 229 metres (750 feet) across at the top, and its construction consumed about a quarter of a million cubic metres of concrete. I doubt that it came in the conical, ready-mixed wagons we are used to seeing, but if it did there would have been a row of some 40,000 of them waiting to discharge their loads. There is also a second dam, Bwlch-y-gle, north-west of the point where the Way leaves the B4518 (and crossed by that road). It is earth-made, the natural pass into Y Fan valley having been stopped up with almost 12,000 cubic metres of soil and debris. The Bwlch-y-gle dam is just a plug in the reservoir's bath – the main dam serving to regulate the flow of Afon Clywedog and, hence, the Severn. It is that purpose which explains the odd design. The slatted front of the spillway deflects water into the side channels and, in them, away from the dam's foundations. Without them the water might wear away the dam's base.

The scheme in the Clywedog valley was high-tech: computer-aided design of the dam, use of hydro-electric generators in the dam structure to power valves, calculations on volume capacity to ensure adequate flow in the Severn at all times but to allow the reservoir to catch flood waters – like a bucket under a leaking roof. But what of the Clywedog valley that lies drowned underneath? No village lies below the surface to emerge at times of drought and haunt the designers, as happens at Efyrnwy and, more spectacularly, at some other reservoirs. During severe droughts all that is revealed is a

114

brown tide-mark. What was swallowed here was good farmland, a network of lanes and tracks, and a way of life, though the latter was already under siege. Depopulation had carried on apace for many years. But while this may be true, the use of Welsh water to quench the thirst of the English Midlands is an emotive issue: the reservoirs of the Elan valley, and on Afonydd Claerwen, Clywedog and Efyrnwy are still regarded as the last nails in the coffins of these rural areas. They also continue to be regarded as open sores.

From the south-western end of the dam, Glyndŵr's Way continues along the minor road that runs towards and along the southern edge of the reservoir. To the left at (908 869) is Pen-y-gaer, the fort in question being an Iron Age hill-fort. The oval enclosure here is stone-walled, an unusual survival, though there are in fact a couple of others in old Montgomeryshire. At the southern end the walls have been crossed at an angle to form a doorway at once defensible and difficult to attack. The massiveness of the walls, some twelve feet (3.6m) thick, is impressive.

Close to a white house the Way turns right, off the road, following the water's edge for a while and passing the local sailing club before rejoining the road. Cross and continue on a track through the Hafren Forest. There are 50 square kilometres (almost 20 square miles) of forest, as many as fifteen million trees. And yet in 1937 there were none. In very ancient times there may have been forest here – though of broad-leaf trees, not conifers – but when planting started there was open moor. In its way the forest has had a more dramatic effect on the area than has the Clywedog reservoir which it dwarfs. The name Hafren is the Welsh name for the Severn. According to legend, Hafren (or Habren) was the daughter of Locrinus, King of Britain, and his true love Estrildis. But Locrinus was married to Gwendolen, daughter of the King of Cornwall, and when he left her for Estrildis she raised an army in Cornwall and returned looking for revenge. In the battle which followed Locrinus was killed.

Gwendolen seized Estrildis and her daughter and threw them into the river to drown, realising too late that it was no fault of Hafren and she should be honoured as her dead father's daughter. In remorse, Gwendolen named the river for the girl. The Romans came and called the River Sabrina, their aspirant being 's' not 'h', and from that came Severn.

Within the confines of the forest there is wildlife - the birdlife includes crossbills and goldcrests, while the animals include the rare and elusive pine marten - but the chief effect of all those trees is to have maintained the high Pumlumon wilderness by limiting access to it. As a result the moor is a wonderful place with a whole array of moorland birds to add to those that exist at the forest boundary and on the well-protected banks of Afon Hafren.

The Way climbs into the Hafren Forest, then descends from it to cross Afon Biga, using the minor road beside the reservoir which has been used and crossed before. Another forest track now cuts off a corner of the road, rejoining it for the final section of walking through the forest. Soon after leaving the forest, turn left along the track for Nant-yr-hafod and continue along field paths to Llwyn-y-gog Farm. To the north-east from here is the scattered hamlet of Staylittle, once a well-known stop on a drovers road. The hamlet is reputedly named either because the drovers rarely stayed more than a single night or from the speed of work of the local blacksmith during the nineteenth century, so speedy at shoeing a horse that a rider had only to stay-a-little. The Welsh name for the hamlet is Penfforddlas, the head of the green road.

From Llwyn-y-gog, the Way continues north and then north-west to reach the ridge of Llechwedd Du, climbing steadily along it to reach the high point of Penycrocbren. The track we are now following is a very ancient one. The Roman fort on Penycrocbren almost certainly means it is at least as old as the Roman occupation of Wales, and as high ridges were the safest way to travel in earlier times - when the valleys were wooded

116

and home to dangerous animals - it is probably older. Later the track was the turnpike road that linked Machynlleth to Llanidloes. On the track the view north is superb, so good that a detour down a rising path from the plateau below the final climb is worthwhile for a closer look.

If the detour is taken the Wayfarer will see Ffrwd Fawr and the head of the valley of Afon Twymyn. Dyffryn Twymyn is magnificent, the steep slopes of scree with outcrops of hard sandstone forming the crags of Creigiau Pennant to the west, the eastern slope being just as steep, but more pastoral. And so straight is the valley that the eye can follow it down to its confluence with Cwm Iaen, all with a backdrop of the hills of Nant yr Eira. At this point we are only a matter of 10 kilometres (6 miles) from Llanbrynmair, also on the Way. But do not be tempted to cut out the circuit westward.

The head of Dyffryn Twymyn is geologically very recent for, until the last Ice Age, the river flowed east as it does to Ffrwd Fawr, before going south to join Afon Clywedog. When the ice came, the north-facing valley that stopped south of Pennant became choked, a small glacier formed and this cut the valley head back to intersect Afon Twymyn's course. The river was deflected northward and, more spectacularly, the hard sandstone horseshoe of Ffrwd Fawr was carved, dropping the river 45 metres (150 feet) to its new valley floor. Though not as high as the falls at Llanrhaedr-ym-Mochnant, Ffrwd Fawr is equally fascinating both for its volume of water – the river rises only three kilometres (2 miles) from the fall – and for the impressive sweep of the rock amphitheatre over which the water hurls itself. Above the falls the confluence of the streams that make Afon Twymyn is a beautiful spot with rowan, fern, rock and white water.

To the west of the falls is Dylife. It is difficult now to believe that this village once housed the thousand workers of a lead mine almost as rich as that at Y Fan, and with a longer history of prosperity. It started before Y Fan, though its greatest period

117

came in the third quarter of the nineteenth century when ore production reached 10,000 tons annually. There was high capital investment: a water-wheel fifty foot (15m) in diameter to drain the lower levels; houses, a church and an inn. But there was always a transport problem, ore had to be carried by pack-horse to Derwenlas, many miles to the west, and the mine could not survive a down-turn in lead prices.

Dylife was also the sceen of a dreadful story that was long thought to be myth. A blacksmith at the mine, Sion y Gof – John the Smith – believed his wife had been unfaithful and murdered her. To provide himself with an alibi he also killed his daughter, throwing the bodies down a disused shaft and spreading the story that they had left him. Later the bodies were found and Sion was tried for murder. He was found guilty and sentenced to death. It was customary for the execution to be local and for the body to be gibbeted in an iron case to act as a deterrent to others. As the village's only blacksmith, Sion had to make his own cage, his last work in his chosen profession. When it was completed he was hanged on Penycrocbren, the hill of the gallows. His body hung from the gallows in its gibbet cage until it rotted away. Then the gallows collapsed and the whole was buried in wind-blown soil. The hill name remained, but the story became a legend. Then in 1938 two local men digging on the hill unearthed the cage: the tale had been fact, not story, and the skull in its iron-piece is now in the St Fagan's Museum outside Cardiff.

The story adds to the chill of the wind that sweeps the hill, carrying down the spirit of Sion y Gof to join the ghost of a village and the ghosts of the dead who lie beneath the shattered tombstones of the small cemetery.

Beyond Penycrocbren, the Way bears left (south) and follows the rim of the superb gorge of the infant Afon Clywedog before crossing equally superb moorland to reach a track close to Glaslyn, the blue lake which, legend states, is bottomless. Another detour turns left here, following the track to Cwm

Hyddgen and Pumlumon. Those seeking Glyndŵr should make this detour as it was on these flanks of Pumlumon that he raised his standard, a two-legged golden dragon on a field of white.

The detour is also worthwhile to disprove the bad press Pumlumon has had over the centuries. In the Mabinogion the Round Table Knights Kay and Bedevere sit on Pen Pumlumon Fawr in the 'greatest wind in the world', while an early traveller called Pumlumon a 'sodden weariness'. Thomas Pennant did not even bother to come - 'I was dissuaded from making it a visit, being informed that it was an uninteresting object, the base most extensive, the top boggy and the view over a dreary and almost uninhabited country.' Peacock, the mid-nineteenth-century traveller, talked of anyone venturing out on the hill alone being 'little better than a fool' as he stood a 99-per-cent chance of never being seen again. Peacock had become lost amidst thick black bog puddles that tugged at his legs, spirit and life. But the reputation is not entirely justified and many will conclude that the more accurate description is that of Robert Gibbings who wrote that this 'is the kind of mountain I like ... cliffs, but not formidable ones ... buzzards soaring ... ecstasy unbelievable.'

The Way does not visit Cwm Hyddgen, making for Machynlleth - ignoring Glyndŵr the warrior in favour of Glyndŵr the statesman. From Glaslyn, the Way follows the track northwards, then bears left along a bridleway that takes the flank of Foel Fadian, the highest peak in old Montgomeryshire. On the peak's flank the Way reaches its highest point, though many will not be content with this, climbing to Foel Fadian's summit for a magnificent view to the west and north.

No follow the bridleway above the tremendous gorge of the upper stretches Afon Dulas: the view westward from this point is superb. The route does not follow Afon Dulas, though that too has an appointment to keep in Machynlleth, but follows Nant

Fadian a little way north, descending quickly to reach Nant-y-fyda. From there take the lane to a minor road and follow it, bearing right, uphill. Before reaching Cefnwyrygrug, turn left along a bridleway which soon drops down to reach a minor road in Cwm Dulas. Continue along the road, but soon turn left along another road to reach Cleiriau-isaf from where a path climbs on to Cefn Modfedd. On the ridge the Way turns south, following a track that descends through a forestry plantation to reach a minor road at Talbontdrain. Turn right, but soon turn left, off the road, along a track that soon heads south, climbing, gently at first as it threads through fields, but then more steeply to go through another forestry plantation as it turns west and then north-west, crossing beautiful country with excellent views to reach Bwlch. From there, head north, passing through one more section of forestry. The Way emerges from the forest on to Parc common, heading west with superb views north to Machynlleth and the Dyfi valley. We are descending now, passing the delightful Bryn Glas to reach a minor road. Turn right along this as far as the white cottages of Caer Gybi, set back from the road on the right. Walk past the cottages and take the path that descends the fancifully named Roman Steps to reach the A487. Turn right along the road/roadside path to Plas Machynlleth (Celtica) and follow the signs to the town centre.

Machynlleth to Llyn Erfynwy

As the town where Owain was crowned, and where he held the Parliament during which he laid down his ideas for the social structure of an independent Wales, Machynlleth is the focal point of our journey. It is also a lovely little market town, set at about the last point in Dyffryn Dyfi where the river could be easily negotiated before it flowed into its flood-plain estuary. But the town is well-removed from the river, suggesting that the river was never trusted.

The Romans came this way and had small forts, probably little more than look-out points, on the hills of Wylfa and Bryn-y-gog between which Machynlleth stands. The Roman Steps that Glyndŵr's Way uses to descend into the town may be named for this occupation, but are almost certainly not Roman by many centuries. One visitor to the town in the mid-nineteenth century summed up this period in the town's history in most eloquent style. 'The Romans fortified this place, to keep in awe the mountaineers, who, many centuries after the Romans had quitted our shores for ever, here established themselves and bade defiance to their old enemies the English.'

The town's position on the Dyfi and mid-way between Dolgellau and Aberystwyth has meant that it has always been a centre for local trade. In 1291 Edward I granted a charter to Owain de la Pole, lord of Powys, that he could hold 'a market at Machynlleth every Wednesday for ever, and two fairs every year'. It is too early yet to say if the market will indeed be held for all of that time, but it is still held now – the wide main street, Heol Maengwyn, being filled every week (on Wednesdays) with the travelling stallholders who make Welsh street markets so appealing.

The town is laid out along a formal T, though the right arm of the T now straggles further than the left, towards the railway which arrived in 1863. At the centre of the T is a clock tower reminiscent of that in Knighton, erected in 1874 to celebrate the

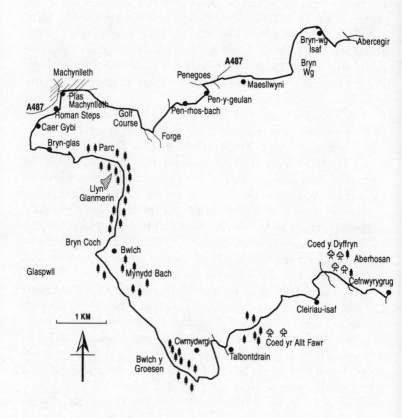

Machynlleth

A487

Plas
Machynlleth
Roman Steps
Caer Gybi

Bryn-glas

Golf
Course

Forge

Pen-rhos-bach

Penegoes

A487

Pen-y-geulan

Maesllwyni

Bryn-wg
Isaf

Abercegir

Bryn
Wg

Parc

Llyn
Glanmerin

Bryn Coch

Glaspwll

Bwlch

Mynydd Bach

Coed y Dyffryn

Aberhosan

Cefnwyrygrug

Cleiriau-isaf

1 KM

Cwmydwrgi

Bwlch y
Groesen

Talbontdrain

Coed yr Allt Fawr

122

coming of age of Viscount Castlereagh, eldest son of the Londonderry family whose mansion was Plas Machynlleth.

The Plas now houses Celtica, which explores the Celtic/Welsh world with the aid of state-of-the-art audio-visual techniques. The centre also holds many exhibitions and has a playroom for younger visitors, a shop and a tea room. Part of the parkland which once surrounded the Plas has been taken over by the town's leisure centre, but enough trees and rhododendrons survive to give an impression of its quality.

Elsewhere, the chief architectural interest in the town lies in its associations with the history of Wales. In Royal House – or at a house on that site – to the north of the Clock Tower, Dafydd Gam was allegedly imprisoned after his failed attempt to kill Glyndŵr. It is not named from that event, but from its use by Charles I in 1644 when the town lay on his route to Chester. And at the end of the lane beside Royal House is Garsiwn (Garrison) Well, where the soldiers of the Earl of Richmond drank on 11 August 1485. The earl stayed at Mathafarn, which the Way passes. His army was en route for Bosworth Field, where on 22 August the army of Richard III was defeated. The earl became Henry VII and so the Tudor dynasty began.

On the northern side of Maengwyn Street is Owain's Parliament House. The present building, in dour stone and slate, is younger than the required date for Owain's Parliament (it probably dates from the late 15th century), and it is by no means certain that it lies at precisely the right point. But tradition places the site here, and the building bows to this tradition with its 1404 Parliament House plaque and exhibition on Glyndŵr and the revolt, both of which are well presented in panels and tableaux. All walkers of the Way should spend time here: the building alone is worth the visit and the exhibition is excellent.

Beside the Parliament House the Tudor-style building – but very recent, in fact 1911 – houses the local Tourist Information Office. Further east, and on the southern side of the street, is another timber-framed building. This one is dated 1628 by inscription and, though it has been much renewed, it is a rare example of such a style of building in this part of Wales.

For the rest the town is Victorian. The church is interesting by virtue of being very English in appearance for a spot buried so deep in Wales. Inside it appears wide, having no colonnades, but the brightly painted wall and ceiling traceries do not seem right, even if they do hark back to pre-Puritan days when all churches were painted. Close to the church is Y Tabernacl which now houses the Museum of Modern Art, Wales. This is a superb place, the tabernacle being a magnificent chapel with an amphitheatre of seating which is now used for concerts, while the galleries exhibit the work of contemporary Welsh artists.

One last treasure of the builder's art is Pontarddyfi (bridge), about 800 metres north of the town. Since the reason for the town's existence is that the river could be crossed here for the last time on its journey to the sea, there has probably been a bridge over Afon Dyfi for many centuries, though the first record is for one built in 1533 for £6 13s 4d. The present bridge, an elegantly low, arched structure, dates from 1805 when its £250 construction cost was shared by the counties of Trefaldwyn (Montgomeryshire) and Meirionnydd which it linked.

Though Afon Dyfi downstream of the bridge becomes increasingly wide and tidal, it is still surprising to discover that at Derwenlas about three road kilometres (2 miles) away - though twice that distance by river - from Machynlleth, there was a port. Derwenlas served Machynlleth's cloth industry as well as the slate quarries of Corris and the lead mines of Dylife. Machynlleth's wool was taken to Ireland, where it was exchanged for flax. If there was no return cargo, soil ballast would be taken on board and this would be dumped on the Dyfi banks. The absence of snakes in Ireland led to the belief that Irish soil somehow repelled reptiles. Goodrich Castle in the lower Wye Valley had a floor of Irish soil to stop toads, and here

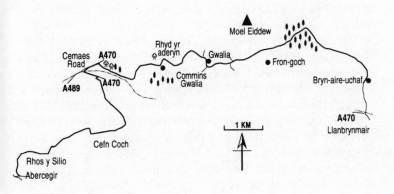

the local farms were advertised as snake-free if they had Irish soil dumped on their land. Strangely, they do actually appear to be snake-free.

Glyndŵr's Way leaves Machynlleth along Maengwyn Street. Turn right beyond Parliament House, following the mountain road for Llyn Clywedog and Llanidloes (also signed for Forge/Aberhosan/Dylife) across the golf course to reach the tiny village of Forge. Follow the road across the bridge over Afon Dulas, then turn left along a minor road (unsigned, just after the last house on the left), heading north-east, but soon turning right again along a path which is followed past Penrhos-bach and Pen-y-geulan to reach the Felin Crewi Water Mill in Penegoes. Until 1999 this was the last working water mill in Wales, but has now closed.

The impressive church in Penegoes has an elegant slate tablet which records that Richard Wilson, the famous landscape artist, was born in the village in 1713. Wilson's father was rector of the church, though the St Cadfarch's that we now see replaced the medieval church at which he officiated in 1880.

Turn right (east) along the pavement of the A489, taking great care as this is a busy road, especially in summer. After about 300 metres, ignore the first turning to the right, but take the second (unsigned, just after 'Tŷ'r Efail') following the lane and the bridleway at its end eastwards, then a path north around the common land of Bryn Wg. From the high point on the northern flank of the hill there are superb views of Dyffryn Dyfi and the hills around Cadair Idris. Now follow the track as it descends into Abercegir, which is entered past the ruin of a flannel factory that was water-wheel powered. Abercegir has a neatness that implies a real care for house and garden, and a quiet calm that makes the heart ache to be part of the community that generates it.

The route from the mill ends in Abercegir's main street. Go left and then sharply back right at the Y-junction to reach a bridleway that heads north, passing Fron Fraith and climbing around the steep sided hill of Rhos y Silio to reach ruinous Gader-goch. The Way now continues along a track with more superb views of Dyffryn Dyfi to the north, eventually reaching a minor road. Turn left and follow this, and them a path to the right, to reach the scattered hamlet of Glantwymynd (Cemmaes Road.)

Across Afon Dyfi from this point is Mathafarn. Though the house that now stands there is from the early seventeenth century, an earlier one on the same site has a place in history. It was owned by Dafydd Llwyd ap Llywelyn, a 'great poet and scholar' who was well-known as an astrologer when, in 1485, Henry, Earl of Richmond stayed the night on his way to Bosworth Field. Henry asked Dafydd if he was going to win the coming battle and Dafydd asked for the night to ponder. Dafydd was deeply troubled, presumably because there was no outcome to his ponderings, and his wife asked him why. When she heard the reason she was furious – not that her prophet-husband could not read the future, but that he was so lacking in common sense. Her solution was obvious – tell Henry he would win, then if he did the Llwydiaid would find favour: if Henry did not win, he was hardly likely to survive long enough to come back and complain. Dafydd did as she suggested. Henry was delighted with the prediction, and 'borrowed' Dafydd's horse. After all, if the battle was to be won he would be able to return it. Henry did win and Dafydd was rewarded, though whether or not the new king returned the horse, history does not reveal. The Welsh drew a moral from the story – 'Gynghor gwraig heb ei ofyn' which, roughly translated, reads 'the unsought advice of your partner is worth taking'.

Glyndŵr's Way crosses Afon Twymyn, that has come from Ffrwd Fawr, and turns right (south-east) immediately on to a lane through a superb piece of oak-woodland and out on to a bridleway between high ferns beside the railway line. Follow the bridleway past Pant-y-no and on to Rhyd yr aderyn. The Way continues along the bridleway, climbing around Commins

Gwalia to reach a minor road. Turn right, but soon go left (east) along an enclosed lane to reach another minor road. Turn left, but soon go right along a bridleway which climbs along the southern flank of Moel Eiddew and then through a forestry plantation. At the far side of the plantation turn right along the forest edge, still climbing at first, but then descending to reach the plantation corner. Now bear left (south-east) away from the forest and follow a broad ridge, with beautiful views down into the valley of Afon Twymyn, and of Llanbrynmair, the next village along the Way. The path emerges on to the access lane for Bryn-aire-uchaf. Turn right along this, following it down into Llanbrynmair.

Here, in the seventeenth century, lived a small colony of Flemish weavers who came to start a wool trade, and succeeded despite having to pack-horse their wool over the high moorland to the north and on to Welshpool. The weavers were latecomers, for high on Newydd Fynyddog to the south of the village are two stone circles. They are beautifully sited, and such sites are so evocative: to be alone with them as the wind stirs the coarse hill grass is to feel the tug of the past. One circle is Lled Croen yr Ych, the width of the skin of the ox. Since such sites have always been tantalisingly mysterious, a local legend grew up that once in the valley there were two giant oxen who were eventually separated (but why?) on to hills on either side of the valley. There, alone but in view of each other, they bellowed in despair until they died. The larger one here on Newydd Fynyddog was skinned and its skin was pegged out to show later generations its true size.

Such folk stories are numerous in the Llanbrynmair district, which also abounds in odd cures and superstitions. Hereabouts if you came face to face with a frog or toad you had to close your mouth, because if it counted your teeth they would fall out. Warts were cured by leaving white pebbles in a parcel at a cross-roads; the finder would open the parcel, take out the stones and transfer the warts to himself. The locals cut their nails on a

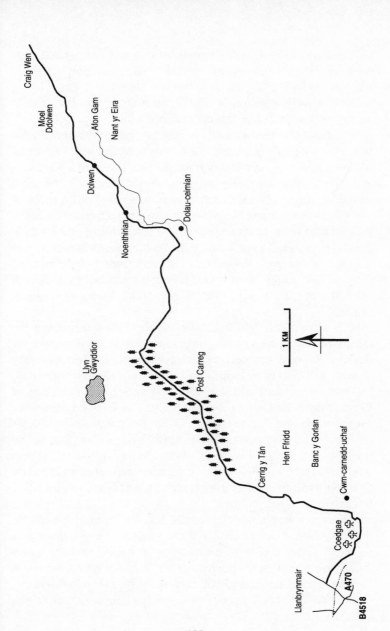

Craig Wen

Moel
Ddolwen

Afon Gam

Nant yr Eira

Dolwen

Noenthirian

Dolau-ceimian

Llyn
Gwyddior

Post Carreg

Cerrig y Tân

Hen Ffridd

Banc y Gorlan

Cwm-carnedd-uchaf

Coedgae

Llanbrynmair

A470

B4518

1 KM

129

Monday so as to retain their complexions and figures and they sang May carols, sometimes coupled with maypole dancing. The carols were sung outside houses, *canu dan y pared* (sung under the wall) a custom so old – and probably pagan – that it had no folk memory or legend attached to it.

But most interesting of all was their name for the 'man in the moon' – *y dyn a'r baich drain*, the man with the load of thorns, sentenced to exile on the moon for picking sticks on a Sunday – and *clwy'r edau wlan*, the 'woollen thread disease'. The local conjuror, effectively the witch-doctor, measured out a piece of yarn three times along the patient's arm from elbow to the tip of the middle finger. This yarn he wound around the patient's neck and then repeated a spell. The yarn was then remeasured twice: if it had shortened, the patient suffered from woollen thread disease, and could be cured by taking two draughts daily of a medicine of saffron with beer or gin, divided into seven equal portions.

Glyndŵr's Way leaves Llanbrynmair northwards along the minor road just beyond the Wynnstay Arms (and signed for Pandy). Beyond the railway it leaves the road, turning right along a path that heads south-east at first, parallel to the railway, but then turns north along a bridleway that climbs the ridge of Esgair Fraith. During pauses for breath, look back for another excellent view of Llanbrynmair. Continue along the bridleway, reaching a forestry plantation beyond Cerrig y Tân. Follow the bridleway through this large plantation, eventually reaching open land by Graig lwyd. The bridleway now descends gently to reach a minor road in the beautiful Cwm Nant yr Eira. Turn left along the road.

There is something very special about following Afon Gam through Cwm Nant yr Eira. The river and the empty moorland to the horizon give a size to nature: it seems that the moor spreading evenly to the horizon must go on for ever. I can come here again and again, and still be thrilled by the barrenness.

At (964 066) the road passes a lonely chapel. To come here,

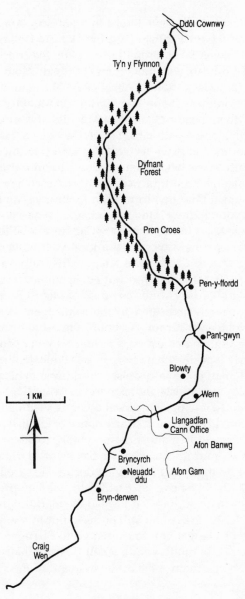

Ddôl Cownwy

Ty'n y Ffynnon

Dyfnant
Forest

Pren Croes

Pen-y-ffordd

Pant-gwyn

Blowty

Wern

1 KM

Llangadfan
Cann Office

Afon Banwg

Bryncyrch

Afon Gam

Neuadd-
ddu

Bryn-derwen

Craig
Wen

131

the locals must have believed hard in their God. After another 1.5 kilometres (about a mile) of road walking, a lane on the left is taken to Dolwen farm. From there a path goes out on to the moor we have been watching from the road. Now for three kilometres (2 miles) that moor is real. Navigation is easy, following a bridleway below the hill-fort on Moel Ddolwen (to the south), then heading north-east across the moor before turning north along a path which skirts the edge of farmland to reach a minor road at Bryn-derwen. The road is followed briefly to reach a path on the left, which is followed across another road to reach Bryncyrch. Continue northwards to reach a minor road. Turn right and follow this to reach a footbridge, on the right, that crosses Afon Banwy into Llangadfan.

The village takes its name from St Cadfan, one of the earliest Celtic saints, and there was once a local well named for him with healing waters. Cadfan was later the first Abbot at Bardsey Island, where 20,000 saints were buried: in medieval times three pilgrimages to Bardsey were the equal of one to Rome. In the yard of the church dedicated to the saint, there lies William Jones, an eighteenth century 'scholar, philosopher and poet'. This is not a unique dedication, but Jones does appear to have been a fairly special character, a self-educated man who translated Roman poets into Welsh. In addition to his poetry he wrote articles on Welsh independence, which he fervently supported, and drew up some local pedigrees with a fine touch of xenophobia – 'I shall not take any notice of English pedigrees, lest I should trace their mushroom nobility to some bastards, arrant thieves, murderers, whether Saxon or Norman.' Jones was also a self-taught and self-styled doctor. He cured scrofula, and if asked to show a certificate which proved his qualifications to do so, showed instead the marks of the disease on himself! Jones' grave can still be seen, but to see one of the best houses of Llangadfan you must go to St Fagan's outside Cardiff, where Abernodwydd, a small thatched hall, has been re-erected. On the main A458 at the east end of the village the

Cann Office Hotel is a famous old coaching inn, its curious name being a bastardised English form of Cae'n y ffos.

To leave Llangadfan, take the minor road opposite the footbridge you crossed to enter the village, following it for 400 metres, then turning left towards Blowty Farm. From the farm, follow field paths to reach a minor road near Bryngwalia. Turn left to a road junction. Here, go straight across, following a track northwards to reach a road at Pen-y-ffordd. Again go straight across and follow a bridleway and track through forestry, part of the vast Dyfnant forest. Within the forest the Way is straightforward, leaving the Wayfarer to spot the birdlife, which includes pied flycatchers, tree pipits, siskins and crossbills. Follow the track through a plantation, then along the forest edge, then through further forestry to reach 'Five Ways'. Here, continue north along a forest road and then descend along a grass track and another forest road to reach Dyfnant. The Way now follows the edge of a field, descending to cross a stream, before re-entering the forest to reach a road. Follow this into the hamlet of Ddôl Cownwy.

Pass the caravan site and cross the bridge, turning left, but soon right along a forest track. The track passes Bryn Cownwy, climbing steeply, then turning left to emerge from the forest on to the hillside above Llyn Efyrnwy (Lake Vyrnwy). The view across the reservoir from here is superb. Now follow the field edge path to reach a track (from the forest on the right) and follow the track to reach Llanwddyn.

Llyn Erfynwy to Welshpool

In 1760 a Mr Probert proposed a scheme to drain the Llanwddyn Bog that lay around the village in the upper reaches of Cwm Efyrnwy. He was convinced that the bog, about five kilometres (3 miles) long and 800 metres wide, could be turned into quality agricultural land. His scheme never came to anything, but a century later someone else was interested in the bog. However, Liverpool Corporation did not want to drain the bog, far from it, they wanted to use the water-bearing qualities to supply their thirsty city. In 1880 work on a dam began at the narrow eastern valley end, where a natural rock barrier was augmented by loose stone with a cement binder. The dam was no feat of modern engineering as at Clywedog. Here, though the roadway is elegant on its thirty-three arches and the spillway nicely faced, the dam is just a plug. Half a million tons of rock infill were used, with 27,000 tons of cement. The dam holds back a reservoir of over 60 thousand million litres (13 thousand million gallons) of water, a lake with a surface area of about 440 hectares (1,100 acres). It supplies water at a rate of around 200 million litres (50 million gallons) daily.

The reservoir brought fresh water to Liverpool, reducing deaths from cholera, but there was a cost. There were about four hundred and fifty people living in the valley, mostly at Llanwddyn village about three kilometres (2 miles) up-valley of the present dam. To re-house them the Corporation took the remarkable action of re-siting the village, moving houses and even headstones and grave remains. The new village was sited beyond the dam and given the same name. It was an inspired answer to a human problem – and a by-product was that they moved the bodies closer to heaven, even if only by a metre or so.

When the Efyrnwy reservoir was constructed it was fashionable to plant the valley sides with conifers. There were several reasons for this. It was thought that the trees generated clouds and so enhanced rainfall, and that they helped prevent

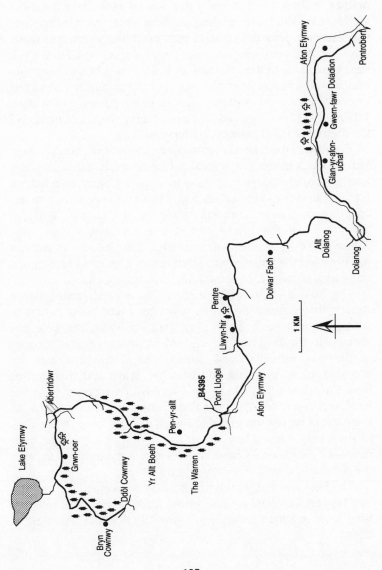

contamination of the water supply. It is now considered that neither of those ideas holds water as well as the lake does, but the trees are still there, lending an air of secrecy and intimacy to the reservoir. This air is further enhanced by the turreted water tower on the northern lake edge, a miniature of Castell Coch near Cardiff, or of the originals for both – the Rhineland castles. The tower, another inspired piece of planning, is a straining tower where water is filtered before being passed to the three 1.07 metre (42-inch) aqueducts which carry the water on its 110 kilometre (70 mile) journey to Merseyside.

Because of the lake's air of mystery, it is natural to add a local fairy story. A mischievous local goblin or spirit, Ysbryd Cynon, was eventually prayed down into a quill feather and hidden under a stone at Llanwddyn. Sadly this fact was forgotten and one day the reservoir-makers blew up the stone, Carreg yr Ysbryd. From the smoke and debris emerged a large frog, rubbing its eyes as if from a long sleep. It hopped away and has not troubled the valley since, although on some nights there is a noise as if someone, or something, is dragging chains.

The lake is encircled by a road that is rarely more than a stone's throw from the water, allowing every combination of sunlight and tree-shade to play their colouring tricks on the surface. In the long drought of 1984 the most westerly sections of the lake retreated, and though old Llanwddyn was not revealed, there were old and bleached walls and tree-stumps near Pont Eunant, sticking up like fossilised bones from the hard, cracked mud. Also near Pont Eunant is a road that crosses a section of barren moorland to Bwlch y Groes. Here, at the Pass of the Cross – legendary site of the saving of a traveller from robbers by a ghostly Christian – there is a magnificent view of the Arannau, a wall of mountains westward.

The lake and the surrounding forest is excellent for birdlife. The lake species can be viewed from three hides: if you have the time look out for goosanders – saw-billed ducks that nest in trees.

Glyndŵr's Way leaves Llanwddyn along the minor road which heads east from the southern end of the Efyrnwy dam, passing the information centre and following a track at its end to descend to Pont Bryn-y-fedwen over Afon Efyrnwy. Cross the bridge to reach Abertridwr and turn right along the road (the B4393). Where the road turns sharply left, continue along the minor road ahead, soon bearing left along a forestry road. Follow this to a minor road. Cross and continue along a track which climbs steeply through the forest, crossing the summit of Yr Allt Boeth. Emerging from the forest the Way follows paths downhill, with excellent views eastwards to Cwm Efyrnwy valley. Follow the paths into Pont Llogel. To the right here is Llwydiarth Park, once home of the influential Welsh family of Fychan. Sir Gruffudd Fychan was one of Glyndŵr's allies in the revolt.

Follow the road southwards through the village, then take the beautiful path heading south-east beside Afon Efyrnwy. The Way leaves the river along field paths heading north-east to reach a minor road. Cross and follow the path opposite to Llwyn-hir and on to another road at Pentre. Turn right, crossing Nant Llwyn-hir and going steeply uphill to a sharp right bend. Here, turn left along a lane, following it for about one kilometre (a little over 0.5 miles) to reach a right turn along a path. Head south along this path: to the right after about a kilometre (0.6 miles) is Dolwar Fach, the childhood home of the late-eighteenth century hymn writer Ann Griffiths.

When the path reaches a road, continue along it briefly, then bear left along a path that climbs on to the flank of Allt Dolanog. There are excellent views as the path rounds the hill before descending to reach a minor road: follow this into Dolanog, a sprawling village, but beautifully set on Afon Efyrnwy. In the lower part of the village an old bridge, with even older safety rails, crosses the water from a huddle of houses. Further upstream the river tumbles over a waterfall that is in part man-made, in part natural cascade, and all very picturesque. The weir once drove a water-wheel for a grain and fulling mill that still stands, though it is now a private house.

From Dolanog, Glyndŵr's Way crosses Afon Efyrnwy, then turns left along the B4382 to reach a path, on the left, which leads to the riverbank. The Way now follows the river closely as it swings around the base of Pen-y-berth. The hill was famous for its springs which were believed to cure eye disorders. The path is a delight, the river well set off by the wooded northern bank. The path leaves the river to reach Gwern-fawr, from where a track is followed all the way to Pontrobert.

The hamlet's name is from the bridge over Afon Efyrnwy, itself named after Oliver ap Robert who, in 1670, was the first to bridge the river at this point. Do not miss the cruck-framed cottage. Go over Oliver's bridge and turn right, then go left after the chapels, passing the Royal Oak Inn. Turn right along the no through road for Bryn-y-fedwen and continue along the track ahead. To the south from here is Dolobran Hall, home of the local family of Lloyds whose small banking business has grown into a household name. The Lloyds were Quakers and east of the hall is a Quaker meeting hall in which, it is thought, William Penn preached before leaving for America and the founding of Pennsylvania.

South-east of Dolobran Hall, on the other side of Afon Efyrnwy is Mathrafal which is strongly believed to have been the site of the court of the princes of Powys, who moved here to escape the border incursions of the Mercian Saxons when their court was at Shrewsbury. The site was used until the twelfth century, when Gwenwynwyn moved his court to the stronger Powys Castle. After the prince had departed, it remained a fortress, finally being totally destroyed by King John in his campaign against Llywelyn Fawr.

The Way now follows delightful field paths to reach a minor road near Coed-cowrhyd. Follow the road to a junction and walk ahead to reach a distinctive right-hand bend. Here, turn left along a path which follows the western flank of Gallt yr

Ancr to reach a minor road. Turn right and follow the road into Meifod.

Dyffryn Meifod is formed between the Broniarth Hills to the south-east and Allt Main and Gallt yr Ancr to the north-west. Though it is, in fact, just a part of the valley of Afon Efyrnwy, it has a distinct identity separate from that of the valley running down from Llyn Efyrnwy itself. A short distance upstream the river has turned sharply northward, giving the vale its southern end, and in the vale it runs in a wide flat plain: there is even an ox-bow lake, almost perfectly horseshoe-shaped – a geography teacher's dream. For a long time the special nature of the Vale has been noted. Cynddelw, a late-twelfth-century bard, loved the grandeur of Gwynedd and 'the spot whose surface is trodden by the brave'. But the vale was 'A privileged sanctuary, a bright cultivated spot – Fair Meifod'. Six centuries later Sion Ysgrifen referred to 'Meifod's Vale most fair'.

The name is not well understood: it could just mean summer pasture but is almost certainly pre-Christian, for Meifod was an important site in the Celtic Christian church and would have adopted a *llan* name if it had not had a name already. The site was chosen by St Gwyddfach and the first church built here was dedicated to him. A second was built later, dedicated to the better known St Tysilio, a son of Brochfael Ysgythrog, Prince of Powys. At that time Meifod was the foremost church of Powys and the princes were buried in it. Within the present church, St Mary's, is an old inscribed stone believed by some to be a monument to a later prince, Madog ap Maredudd. If it is Madog, who died around 1160, then it dates from the time of the first construction of the present church. Some experts, however, believe that the stone is much older, perhaps as early as the ninth century, pointing to the Vikingesque style of some of the carvings in support of this theory.

The churchyard covers nine acres, encompassing the sites of the two earlier churches and a great deal more besides. With the wide street outside and the far-flung houses, it gives Meifod a roominess unlike other Welsh villages. The dominance of the huge church site is an indication of the importance that spirituality has always played in Meifod's history.

The Way leaves Meifod by following the main road through the village and turning left along the minor road that crosses Broniarth Bridge over Afon Efyrnwy. Bear left with the road, staying close to the river and then turning right along a path which climbs through the forest on Broniarth Hill. Where it emerges from the trees the Way is above Llyn Du, a small stretch of water but a magic stretch, reputedly unfathomable. Turn right along a minor road, bearing left at a junction, then turning left to Tŷ-newydd.

A little further along the road, to the right, below the afforested hill fort, is Cobham's Garden where in 1417 Sir John Oldcastle, Lord Cobham, was captured. Cobham was a Hereford man who served Henry IV and Henry V loyally and bravely in battle, but unfortunately he was a Lollard, a follower of John Wycliffe and his outlawed religious sect. As a result Cobham was imprisoned in the Tower, but escaped in 1413 and came to the Meifod area where he sheltered with Lollard friends in the woods. Many knew where they hid, but no one would say until someone betrayed them for the thousand-mark reward that Henry V was offering for their capture. Cobham was taken at his 'Garden', though he put up strong resistance during which his leg was broken, apparently by a local woman, using a stool. Cobham might have escaped but for the break: as it was he was taken to London where he was tried and condemned. He was dragged on a hurdle to St Giles' Field and hanged from a gallows by a chain around his waist over a slow fire which consumed both him and the gallows.

From Tŷ-newydd, the Way follows field paths south to reach a minor road near Bwlch Aeddan. Continue southwards along the road, but soon turn left along a path to Pant Farm and on to a minor road opposite Stonehouse Farm. Go through the farm to reach another minor road. Turn left and follow the road for 500

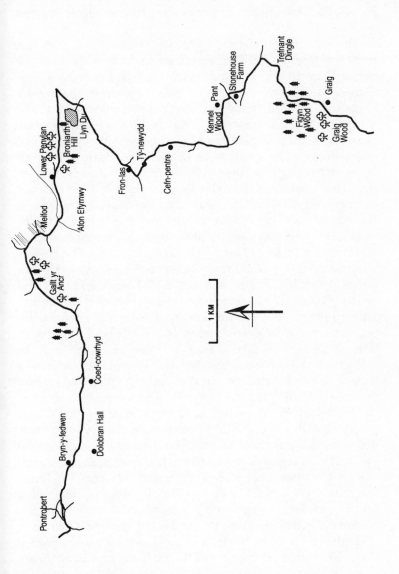

1 KM

Pontrobert
Bryn-y-fedwen
Dolobran Hall
Coed-cowrhyd
Gallt yr Ancr
Meifod
Afon Efyrnwy
Lower Penylan
Broniarth Hill
Llyn Du
Fron-las
Tŷ-newydd
Cefn-pentre
Kennel Wood
Pant
Stonehouse Farm
Trefnant Dingle
Figyn Wood
Graig
Graig Wood

metres, then turn right along the access lane to Lower Trefnant Farm.

The Way now climbs steeply through Figyn Wood, emerging from the woodland to fine views southwards. Follow a path downhill past Graig and through Graig Wood to reach a lane. Cross and follow a path southwards to reach a minor road. Cross this and follow the northern edge of a golf course and then climb to the summit of Y Golfa, the final peak on the walk. From the summit a path heads east, passing Pen-y-golfa and going through the grounds of Llanerchydol Hall, a Regency Tudor reworking of a house built in 1776, but on a very ancient site. This final section of the Way is through very pleasant country and it is with surprise that the Wayfarer arrives at Welshpool, reaching Raven Square and the terminus of the Welshpool and Llanfair Railway, one of the steam-hauled narrow-gauge railways for which Wales is famous. The railway was opened in 1903 after many years of clamouring by Llanfair Caereinion which had missed out in 1854 when a railway had linked Oswestry, Welshpool and Newtown. At the time a railway, the great modern invention, was seen as a panacea for economic woes and every market town was anxious to have its line. The line was finally axed in 1956, but taken over by enthusiasts who have renovated the system and operate a regular schedule from late April to early October. The journey from Welshpool to Llanfair takes about fifty minutes.

Welshpool (Y Trallwng) is another 'gateway to Wales', though one that because of its position on the Severn is more deserving of the name than most. In appearance it is a Georgian market town, arguably more English than Welsh, an assessment at odds with that of Leland who in the reign of Henry VIII found the town 'wel buildid after the Walsch fashion', but finding favour with Defoe who found it a 'good fashionable place and has many English dwelling in it and some very good families'.

In the centre of the town there is a house with an inscription that tells us that an ancestor of the builders, one Roger Jones, was in the reign of Edward IV the first Jones in Wales. Elsewhere the church of St Mary (or St Cynfelyn) is worth a visit. Adam of Usk was priest here in 1411 and William Morgan, translator of the Bible into Welsh, was vicar from 1575-8. The church has some 13th century features, but is chiefly of interest for the odd alignment of the tower and nave with the chancel. Some experts believe this may have due to rebuilding work required after the Glyndŵr rebellion during which the church was extensively damaged.

Powys Castle is now administered by the National Trust: the castle was given to the nation in 1952 in lieu of death duties but has been continuously occupied by members of the royal house of Powys and then the Earls of Powys for over seven hundred years. Originally there was a motte and bailey castle here, the present castle – built of red sandstone and known, not unnaturally, as Castell Coch, the Red Castle – being started near it by Gruffudd ap Gwenwynwyn. Unfortunately Gruffudd was involved in a plot to overthrow Llywelyn Fawr (Llywelyn the Great) and for his pains his castle was destroyed. The present building dates from about 1275, though there have been many additions and alterations since then. When the male line from Gwenwynwyn died out, Hawys, the sister and heir of the last of the line, married John Charleton, a Shropshire man. Charleton lent his bloodhounds to help the search for Cobham, the Hereford Lollard, and was cursed to be unhappy. A gifted hermit was brought to lift the curse, but he could not and Charleton died a miserable man. After his death the castle was owned by more Charletons, then by the Greys and the Herberts. William Herbert held the castle for the Royal cause in the Civil War, but it was taken by the forces of Sir Thomas Myddleton, though Cromwell intervened to stop its demolition by the occupying Roundheads. The castle was restored to the Herberts and passed by the female line to the Clive family, famous for their exploits in India. The castle houses a museum of the Indian collection of the Clives.

Visitors can enjoy not only the architectural beauties and luxurious decorations of the castle itself, but the superb gardens laid out in formal style on seventeenth-century terraces. The terracing did not meet with the approval of 'Capability' Brown, who landscaped the park. He wanted them 'ruggedised' into crags. Pennant was unhappy too: he thought they were in 'imitation of the wretched taste of St Germain en Laye'. It is certainly true that the gardens show both Italian and French influences which would justify the two dissenters, but their opinion seems too harsh as there is much to admire. The huge yews - clipped by hand by a man with a long ladder and a truly unenviable job - are superb, as is the Orangery, and many of the statues are in the original lead. Overall, Powys is a marvellous place and a fitting end point to Glyndŵr's Way, though the true end point is the Pont Howell picnic site beside the canal. Though now part of what became (in 1846) the Shropshire Union Canal, the waterway here was built as the Montgomery Canal linking Newtown to the Ellesmere Canal near Franckton. The canal was the brainchild of Welshpool and Newtown merchants and was completed in 1821, almost thirty years after the formation of the company created to construct it. That is a long time, but it has to be remembered that the canal was dug entirely by hand - by 'navigators', the men who dug 'navigations' as canals were known at the time: the terms has come down to us as 'navvies', a pejorative term for a manual labourer, a far way from the original usage when the men were seen as pioneers. The main trade of the new canal was limestone and coal coming into Wales, with timber being exported. Trade ceased in 1936 when a breach caused the canal to empty. It was not refilled and lay neglected for years. Only in 1969 was restoration work started. Today the canal is a much loved waterway and its tranquil edge is a fitting end point for our walk.

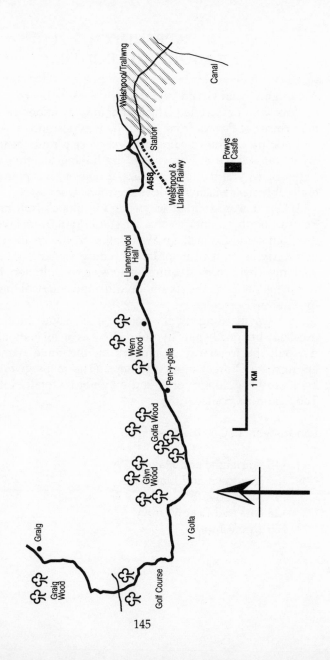

APPENDIX 1:
ABOUT THE ROUTE

Although Owain Glyndŵr eventually took as his coat of arms the four lions of Gwynedd, he fought initially under the arms of the princes of Powys from whom he was descended. After the new county of Powys came into existence a route bearing the great leader's name was created by linking together existing rights of way and minor roads. At one or two points, most noticeably near Machynlleth, major roads were used.

When it was decided to create a National Trail based on Powys County Council's route the statutory powers invested in the Contryside Council for Wales allowed the creation of new public rights of way in order to reduce the amount of road walking. This process required extensive consultation, but was completed by 2000, the six-hundredth anniversary of the start of the Glyndŵr rebellion.

The waymarking on the route is, as would be expected, excellent, but on Owain Glyndŵr's Way as on all National Trails it would be foolhardy to embark on the route without the appropriate Ordnance Survey maps. (The maps given in this book are for guidance only and may not be totally infallible.) The required OS sheets are:

Landranger (1:50,000) series

    148 Presteigne and Hay-on-Wye
    136 Newtown and Llanidloes
    135 Aberystwyth
    125 Bala and Lake Vyrnwy
    126 Shrewsbury

Explorer (1:25,000) series

> 201 Knighton & Presteigne/Tref-y-Clawdd a Llanandras
> 214 Llanidloes & Newtown/Y Drenewydd
> 215 Newtown/Y Drenewydd & Machynlleth
> 239 Lake Vyrnwy/Llyn Efyrnwy & Llanfyllin

These maps do not cover the final 2 or 3 kilometres into Machynlleth (which are on Outdoor Leisure Sheet 23 - Cadair Idris & Bala Lake/Llyn Tegid) and the final kilometre or so into Welshpool (covered on Sheet 216 Welshpool & Montgomery)

APPENDIX 2:
OFFA'S DYKE, THE RETURN JOURNEY

At Welshpool Glyndŵr's Way can be linked to the Offa's Dyke National Trail which, since that route also passes Knighton, allows a continuous route to be made through mid-Wales, virtually from border to sea and back.

To join Offa's Dyke from Welshpool, cross the Shropshire Union Canal on the B4381 and follow that road to Lower Leighton (244 066). Go left and follow this road to (248 076). Here turn right up Hope Lane through the village of Hope, to join Offa's Dyke at (257 073). From Hope, Knighton is about 40kms (about 25 miles). Between the two, the Offa's Dyke Path passes through some very fine countryside, as well as the town of Montgomery.